Ragnhild Silkoset
Pricing

Ragnhild Silkoset
Pricing

—

A Guide to Pricing Decisions

DE GRUYTER

This book is adapted from "Pris. En håndbok i prisbeslutninger" published by Cappelen Damm (Oslo, Norway).

ISBN 978-3-11-099833-7
e-ISBN (PDF) 978-3-11-098710-2
e-ISBN (EPUB) 978-3-11-098711-9

Library of Congress Control Number: 2022946814

Bibliographic information published by the Deutsche Nationalbibliothek
The Deutsche Nationalbibliothek lists this publication in the Deutsche Nationalbibliografie; detailed bibliographic data are available on the Internet at http://dnb.dnb.de.

© 2023 Walter de Gruyter GmbH, Berlin/Boston
Cover image: LordRunar/iStock/Getty Images Plus
Typesettung: Integra Software Services Pvt. Ltd.
Printing and binding: CPI books GmbH, Leck

www.degruyter.com

Preface

One of the most difficult decisions a business manager must make is in pricing their products [1]. If they price too low, they risk not covering the costs or generating profit. If they price too high, they can risk potential customers never becoming paying customers. Important questions in pricing decisions include the following:

- How should I price my products?
- How much will sales change if I increase the price?
- To whom will the product lose market share if I change the pricing?
- What value do the customers put on the different product benefits?

Price is one of the most flexible elements in the marketing mix, and it has a direct effect on the profitability and cost efficiency of a company. However, even though price has a major impact on companies' earnings, it has, until a few years ago, been partly overlooked in academic research [2]. In marketing, we see that the predominant focus is on product innovations, brand building, distribution channels, and communication on social media. Price is treated as the easiest factor to adjust, but unfortunately many price changes are based on intuition, gut feeling, or the marketer's personal experience.

Strategic plans for a company's pricing policy require one to adapt to the competitive situation, the company's profitability targets and sales, long-term survival, flexibility, the company's management structures, the company's strategic objectives, and routines for enforcing price tactics [3].

The purpose of this book on pricing decisions is to present a basic tool for pricing strategy that can be used by students, companies, and entrepreneurs in all phases.

The book starts with the objectives for the pricing strategy for both existing and new products. This is followed by Chapter 2, where I discuss value-based pricing and value-to-customer (VTC). VTC analysis is a useful tool that puts the various price alternatives into a system and coordinates them with the company's overall strategy. Simple calculations are described. The analysis provides a good basis for decision-making for the company's long-term work with pricing strategy. Chapter 3 focuses on practical tools for mapping the different price points. This part is especially important for startup companies and companies that are launching new products in the market. The topic here is more analytical, and I use well-known analysis models to map price alternatives. The analysis is explained using Microsoft Excel (hereafter referred to as "Excel").

Throughout this book, I recommend dynamic pricing, where you vary prices based on the customers' willingness to pay. In Chapter 4, I describe how one can vary the prices for identical products or services, while in Chapter 5 I describe how you can get the same customer to volunteer to pay more for a product. Competition on price can, however, be so intense that it ends up in a price war, and Chapter 6

https://doi.org/10.1515/9783110987102-202

describes how price wars arise, how one should act along the way, and how to prevent a price war. To remind one about the realities, Chapter 7 is devoted to customer reactions to unfair prices. Chapter 8 is devoted to the proper use of price tactics, in terms of sales and discounts, while Chapter 9 describes how the presentation of numbers affects whether products are perceived as good bargains or not. In Chapters 10 and 11, I have written more specifically about pricing strategy for e-commerce and the sharing economy. At the end of the book, chapter 12 includes elementary profitability analysis.

Contents

Chapter 8

Chapter 9

Chapter 10

Chapter 11

Chapter 12

Chapter 1
Objectives for the Pricing Strategy

Introduction

Price is an important tool for a company to achieve its strategic goals. In this chapter, I describe different types of objectives for pricing policy. In times of crisis, the goal may be survival, while in good times, the goal may be growth and increased market share. Another objective may be to calm the competition, while a more aggressive objective may be to remove or take over a competitor. At the same time, there are surprisingly few businesses that are aware of how price strategy can be used to meet the company's strategic objectives.

Choice of Pricing Strategy

The most elegantly stated pricing strategy I know is from IKEA. They state: "*When we design the furniture, we start with the price tag.*" This is an important lesson that many other companies should listen to. Customers value products differently, and the question is *not* how much we have to pay to cover the costs of purchasing or producing the product. IKEA focuses on the costs that can be *defended* given the value and willingness to pay the customer segment has for IKEA's products.

Value-based pricing is often the recommended pricing strategy from a professional point of view (see Figure 1.1). The aim is to ensure customers are satisfied with the price they pay for the product, as well as the company being able to utilize the variation in the market's willingness to pay. To achieve such a pricing strategy, the company must identify which attributes of the products or services create *unique* value for customers. Making a distinction between price, value, and quality is important for handling prices in the correct way. This is because the price should reflect value. Price is often defined as meaning that the customer must *sacrifice* to obtain a product. Value is defined as the customer's assessment of the *usefulness* of a product based on the perception of what you give and what you get in return. Quality, in turn, is about the fulfillment of the product or service *attributes*. The literature claims that a purchase is based on value and not quality. You can't disagree with that. I discuss this in the second chapter of this book.

Cost-based pricing focuses on "fair returns" and hardly at all on the customers themselves [4]. You can easily calculate a multiplicative surcharge on production or purchase cost. This builds improperly on the principle that the costs of production are stable and do not change with sales volume. This leads to underpricing in strong markets and overpricing in weak markets. The paradox with such a strategy is that the less you sell, the higher the unit costs are, and the less competitive you will be.

https://doi.org/10.1515/9783110987102-001

Cost-based pricing – traditional product orientation system

Develop the product	Produce the product	Sell the product
Product design	Bid	Sell product
Process design	Production	Advertise
	Services	PR and promotion
		Price
		Sales and distribution

Value-based pricing – value delivery system

Determine the value	Produce the value	Communicate the value
Understand value drivers	Product and process design	Sales message
Determine target customers	Bid, production	Advertising
Determine benefit, price	Distribution	PR and promotion
	Service	
	Price	

Figure 1.1: Different Objectives with the Pricing Strategy.

Cost-based pricing thus becomes a more reactive pricing strategy, where you do not sit in the driver's seat and lead your own price development.

With *competitor-based pricing*, the company sets the price close to the price of a specific competitor, and preferably a little below if they are a market challenger [4]. Such competitor-based pricing gives the competitor a full deck to play with, and they can control market access exactly as they wish. Lowering prices in markets that are not important to them, for example, forces other companies to earn even less money from these customers. In markets where the company has a clear and strong competitive position, customers will still prefer the competitor even though their prices are higher. Thus, the competitor also succeeds in these customer segments.

In the case of a *customer-based pricing*, the goal is to map the customer's willingness to pay for the product during the purchase process. This is a standard strategy for car dealers, who often operate with a single price on the label for the car, but who have great freedom to lower the price and add additional equipment, all based on the information they pick up on how the customer reacts to the introductory price as well as on their ability to pay [5]. Thus, the realized price can deviate a lot from the actual price. The risk with such a pricing strategy is that the profitability is calculated based on list prices, while the realized prices can deviate a lot from this.

Pricing Strategy Matrix for New Products

A pricing strategy matrix looks at the price profiling of the company at an overall strategic level. The matrix sets guidelines for the customers' perception of the company's products and quality, which in turn affects the willingness to pay for the products (see Figure 1.2). This strategy lays the groundwork for entrepreneurs and for new product launches. Switching between the strategies afterward is difficult as the customers have already established an idea of where the company is in the price-quality map.

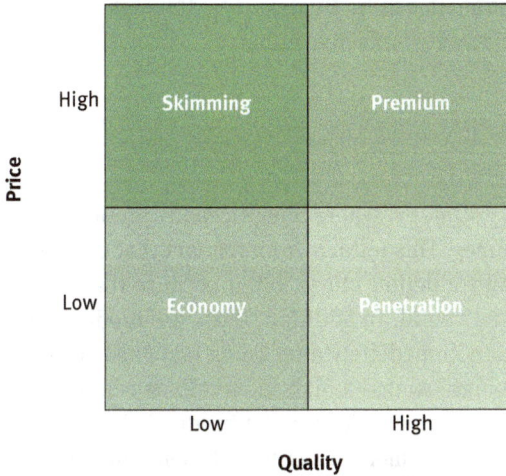

Figure 1.2: Price Strategy Matrix.

Pricing strategy for new products generally follows two paths, namely "product skimming" and "product penetration" [6]. A common mistake many make with innovations and new products is that they start the pricing planning too late. Price should be included as a development criterion at the very beginning of the production process and with the customer's perception of value as a starting point.

Price Skimming Strategy

Price skimming is a demanding strategy as the company positions itself towards a sharp customer segment that requires extraordinary products and extraordinary performance. Prices in such a market are in the upper layer and are made possible through involved and interested customers who have low price sensitivity to new product launches. One example is customers who are particularly interested in fashion, and who are willing to pay high prices to get access to new trends. As the market matures, these garments reach a more price-sensitive market, and one switches to a more volume-based strategy. Another example is technology, where many customers are willing to pay extra for the latest models. The advantage of such a pricing strategy is that it is far easier to reduce the price in the future than it is to increase it.

The advantages of price skimming are that you have a high profit margin and quickly earn the development and production costs. Dealers, however, can also earn quick money and are a driving force in continuing with the strategy. Price skimming creates an experience of high-quality products.

The disadvantage of price skimming is that the competitors can reduce their prices and thus take over large parts of the market. This strategy can succeed only for small-volume sales. Also, former customers can be frustrated by the high introductory price. The strategy is not particularly cost-effective either.

Penetration Pricing Strategy

Penetration pricing follows a contrary strategy, where one prices the product lower than the economic value to the customer. This follows from the fact that customers have a high price sensitivity in the introduction phase, often because the product requires trialing before it is considered useful. In addition, these are products that are often exposed to strong competition immediately after being launched. The production capacity for such products is high, so that a high sales volume can be maintained. Penetration pricing is also used in many phases of a product's life cycle by reducing the price sharply to meet new customer segments and their willingness to pay. Note, however, that a strategy where you reduce the price of products this much can make it difficult to increase the price again later. Correct and good information about customers' price sensitivity is a prerequisite to succeed with this strategy. We also see that it is used in the retail industry: for example, Kroger and Costco implement a penetration pricing strategy for their organic products.

The advantages of penetration pricing include the fact that it reduces the threshold for the customer to be able to start using a product. It decreases and weakens the competition and can be a tool for achieving market dominance.

The disadvantage of penetration pricing is that it rarely succeeds when the competitor has a very strong brand that dominates the market. If prices increase, customers will disappear. The strategy also has a high potential for triggering a price war.

Economy Pricing Strategy

With economy pricing, one provides a low-quality product at a low price. This strategy is often used by companies that sell very similar products without special advantages, such as generic products at retailers. The products have little variation in quality, and the prices are predictable and determined in the market. These are products that have been on the market for a long time, and customers are mostly looking for refills when consumed, or they need some products but are indifferent to which they choose. These are also products that customers do not expect to have for a long time.

The advantage of economy pricing is that this is a safe pricing strategy in turbulent times. Customers want to pay for a minimum, and that's what is delivered. This strategy can also generate higher market shares if you keep the price below the competitors' level.

The disadvantage of economy pricing is that small companies may have difficulty establishing themselves in these markets as they are unable to maintain profitability. Customers are either not seen as loyal or they are looking for the lowest possible price and behave accordingly.

Premium Pricing Strategy

With a premium pricing strategy, the company keeps the prices artificially high with a view to increasing the quality experience for the customers. The products have superior quality or attributes that surpass the quality or attributes of competitors' products. In such markets the customers have strong faith in the high price and high-quality statement. Customers are very quality conscious and have both the willingness and the ability to pay higher prices. One example of a premium pricing strategy is luxury cars, such as Mercedes Benz, Audi, and Tesla.

The advantage of premium pricing is that one can compete fully based on brand and awareness in the market. The brand stands as a quality carrier, and customers have good knowledge about the various providers. The strategy leads to higher profitability.

The disadvantage of premium pricing is the high marketing costs. In addition, there is a limited customer segment, and one constantly risks losing customers.

Different Types of Objectives with the Pricing Policy

These examples of objectives are adapted from Hoch and Rao [3]:

Price-profit satisfaction. Here, the company is interested in keeping prices stable within certain time intervals. This happens across demand changes with the purpose of having a predictable income.

Sales maximization and growth. In this case, the prices are set so that you get the highest possible sales for a product or product line. Here, the price policy satisfies the objective only if the company achieves maximum sales.

Make money. In some industries a company wants to use its positioning to sell products at premium prices to make quick money.

Slow down competition. With this objective for its pricing policy, the company wants to prevent new competitors from entering the market or one wants a predictable competitive situation to optimize the resource usage.

Market share. This pricing policy can be used to increase the company's market share or achieve a leading position in its market.

Survival. In situations with a large degree of uncertainty, such as the coronavirus pandemic, many companies find that the goal of the pricing policy is simply survival. This means that they must endure a lot of defeats and obstacles to maintain their core business.

Market penetration. Some companies want to achieve the highest possible unit sales, often because volume is closely linked to unit costs. This pricing policy is possible with high price sensitivity to new products because customers will respond with increased purchases at reduced prices.

Market skimming. When launching new products, some companies will choose a market skimming policy. In these cases, the company estimates the highest price an innovation can achieve in the market, given the various competitive advantages the product has compared to substitutes (replaceable products).

Early cash recovery. With this price policy the company creates a large and continuing demand for the product with the purpose of gaining quick earnings. With high market uncertainty, you can also accept a relatively low price, so that you have a buffer against future declining demand.

Satisfactory rate of return. Many companies want a pricing policy where they set prices that maximize current profits. They estimate the demand and cost of alternative prices and select the prices that produce the maximum current profit, cash flow, or return on investment.

Development of the Company's Pricing Strategy

Companies that choose to focus on profit maximization risk experiencing bottlenecks in their production and delivery. This in turn can affect sales and delivery. That's why not all products can meet all the objectives set. Some products must be sold with lower margins to achieve market growth, while others will reduce new competition. One set of products can operate in a market with declining demand, while others may experience being replaced with new technology. The most important thing to remember is that a common understanding of the objective of the pricing strategy is necessary for the company's employees to process pricing decisions in the correct way.

In an empirical study, Liozu and Hinterhuber [7] analyzed several hundred industrial companies in over 110 countries and found that the companies' price competence had a strong effect on profitability. They further found that value-based pricing had a direct and positive effect on the companies' profitability, while competitor-based pricing reduced profitability. They tested how various pricing strategies influenced price competence and found that companies that implemented a value-based pricing strategy had a superior effect on their price competence, followed by a weaker effect from cost-based pricing and the lowest effect from competitor-based pricing. The price competence developed, in other words, through the companies' conscious choice of pricing strategy. For those companies that see prices as a lose/win situation between the company and its customers, the research shows that this provides no valuable expertise on prices in the company. Those who focused on continuously finding ways to innovate prices obtained a clear effect on the companies' competitive advantage [8, 9].

To assist in the process of creating a clear pricing strategy, some key questions need to be answered [6]:

1. What is the company's strategy?
2. How does the pricing strategy support or hinder the implementation of the company's other strategies?
3. How does the pricing strategy affect the performance of the other departments in the organization?
4. How do the departments collaborate on the pricing strategy?
5. What effect does the pricing strategy have on the management and leadership of prices in the company?
6. What impact does the pricing strategy have on the company's customers and competitors?

Price policy is about the overall objective and driving rules for the function price has in the company. Price strategy defines the objective and can be developed through following these tips [6]:

1. Ensure that the objective is clearly formulated, measurable, and consistent.
2. When there are multiple targets, make priorities or specify how the objectives are related.
3. Ensure that everyone who makes pricing decisions in the company, at all levels, understands their responsibility within the objective.
4. Understand the consequences of the objective for finance as well as the behavior of the buyers in the market.
5. The more competitors and customers know about the company's pricing strategy, the better.

Transparency prevents misunderstandings and gives the right signals about the long-term intention of the company with its products and services. This is described in Chapter 6 on price competition. In addition, it is important that price decisions are made in consultation with the company's marketing strategy, which in turn is rooted in the company's overall strategy.

Summary

This chapter shows how important it is to coordinate price work so that it helps a company to achieve its strategic goals. As part of this, I have discussed a whole range of different types of objectives a company may have for its pricing policy. I have then described the main attributes of a value-based, competitive, and cost-based pricing strategy. With this I have shown a pricing strategy matrix for brand-new products.

Chapter 2
Value-Based Pricing

Introduction

Value-based pricing is one of the most widely used methods for setting prices for products and services. At the same time, it can be demanding and difficult to achieve in practice [10]. In this book, I go through, step by step, how value-based pricing is implemented. In this review I use VTC analysis (value-to-customer analysis), and I demonstrate a practical example of how to perform a value-based pricing strategy. A VTC analysis consists of five steps, namely customers' perception of value, competing alternatives, product uniqueness, quantification of values, and finally drawing this together into the economic value for customers. VTC analysis ensures a comprehensive understanding of a company's pricing strategy.

Value, Price, and Quality

A Purchase Is Always Based on Value and Never on Price! This statement may seem surprising given that this book is about price. What I mean is that if a consumer perceives that they must *give* more than they *get* from a transaction, they will stop buying. Ergo, if the price is higher than the utility of the product, there will not be any exchange. In other words, the utility describes whether the value is positive. To obtain sales, one must therefore either increase the value or reduce the cost to sell the product. I will go through these important concepts below in more detail.

Perceived value is the consumer's overall assessment of the utility of a product based on the perception of what is received (benefits) and what is given (costs). This means that value is individual and personal. It is a compromise based on what you get versus what you give. For a breakfast juice, perceived value will consist of the attributes of the product (taste, smell, color) and conditions that lie outside the product (prestige, psychological well-being, packaging). The perception of value can also vary depending on where you are in the buying process [11]. At the time of purchase, value can be perceived based on low prices, sales, or discounts. When preparing to buy, value can be perceived based on access to information, assessments, and availability. I discuss this in greater depth in the next section.

Price is defined as what one sacrifices (money, time, risk) to acquire a product. Price in this context is more than the money you pay for a product. For example, on Black Friday, some customers are willing to wait in line for hours to save money on a product. For others, money is less important, and they are not willing to sacrifice this time to acquire a product.

https://doi.org/10.1515/9783110987102-002

Perceived quality is defined as the consumer's assessments of a product's superiority or excellence [11]. This means that quality is not an objective characteristic of a product, but the consumer's interpretation of the utility value.

We can summarize this discussion in an equation where we put the concepts in context.

$$Value = \frac{\text{What you get (functional and emotional benefit)}}{\text{What you sacrifice (time, money, risk)}}$$

When the equation is greater than 0, the customer experiences a positive transaction benefit and will be willing to make a purchase. As previously mentioned, the elements in the equation will be perceived differently between customer groups, situations, over time, and between products. We will discuss this in detail throughout the book.

The matrix in Table 2.1 gives an overview of what the customer sacrifices in a purchase [12]. Customers sacrifice not only the "monetary amount," i.e., dollars and cents, they also sacrifice several more elements in a purchase, such as risk and time. This is important to remember when we investigate further customers' purchase situations.

Table 2.1: Dimensions of Price [12, 13].

	Dimensions of price	
	Effort	**Risk**
Monetary:	Financial – cash – credit – countertrade	Financial – personal – organizational
Nonmonetary:	Time – travel – shopping – waiting – performance	Consequences – social – psychological – physical – functional

Effort	
Financial price	
– cash	Currency, checks, drafts, debit cards
– credit	Credit cards, charge accounts, line of credit, accounts payable
– countertrade	Barter, swap, or trade products
Time	
– travel time	The time it takes to physically get to the store (seller's location)

Table 2.1 (continued)

– shopping time	The time it takes a buyer to search for and evaluate a product
– waiting time	The time it takes a buyer to get checked out of a store, waited on by a salesperson, waited on in a service firm, or to wait for ordered products
– Performance time	The time it takes to use a product or carry out a certain action
– Monitoring time	The time it takes to remember to carry out a certain action
Risk	
Financial risk	
– financial risk	The risk that the product will not be worth the financial price
Consequences	
– Psychological risk	The risk that a poor product choice will harm a consumer's ego
– Physical risk	The risk to the buyer's or others' safety in using products
– Functional risk	The risk that the product will not perform as expected
– Social risk	The risk that a product choice may result in embarrassment before one's friends/family/work group

Benefit

To illustrate the importance of focusing on value, look at the water bottles in Figure 2.1. If you want to satisfy the functional benefit, one liter of Dasani water at Walmart for $1.96 can absolutely be the right decision. However, there are more benefits than the purely functional one customer seeks to satisfy when buying a bottle of water.

In point form we can describe it this way:
– *functional benefit* – you want to quench your thirst
– *social benefit* – you want to signal class affiliation
– *affective benefit* – the personal feeling of consuming
– *recognition* – you want to satisfy personal circumstances, for example being a news seeker
– *hedonistic benefit* – you want to achieve a sense of joy
– *aesthetic benefit* – you want to satisfy the need for style and elegance
– *situational benefit* – satisfaction here and now
– *holistic benefit* – lifestyle and wholeness are in focus

These benefits affect something as simple as one bottle of water varying in price from free to the tap through a few hundred on the bottle and for the most expensive water – Svalbardi. The latter is a 4,000-year-old extra clean water. You get it

Figure 2.1: Water in Many Varieties and Price Ranges.

for $80 for 750 ml. Til is a liter price at $107. However, it is supposed to be possible to get hold of Svalbardi water on Svalbard for only $40 per bottle.

Steps in VTC Analysis

Value-based pricing appeals to those people who want to work actively with pricing strategy, yet it is often misunderstood [14]. One mistake that is often made with this pricing method is confusing *value* and *differentiation value*. Value-based pricing is a strategy where a price is set based on what *separates* (differentiates) the value of our product from the value of competing products. This error or misunderstanding means that many companies either do not utilize their prices optimally or they give up and choose instead cost-based or competitor-based pricing. In Figure 2.2, I illustrate the steps we must use to conduct a VTC analysis for value-based pricing.

Step 1: Determine Customer Segments

At the start of the development of a value-based pricing strategy, you must first decide which customer segment you want to satisfy. Customer segments can vary based on different willingness to pay, given the perception of value and situations. In practice, this means that there are groups of customers who value the attributes of the product differently. In the VTC analysis, you must select one customer segment at a time and run each analysis separately. If you want to serve several customer segments, you must therefore map a value-based price for each individual

Customers	Competitors	Attributes	Customer value	Economic value

Step 1:	Step 2:	Step 3:	Step 4:	Step 5:
Determine customer segments	Map competing players	Map differentiation attributes	Quantify customer value	Calculate total economic value

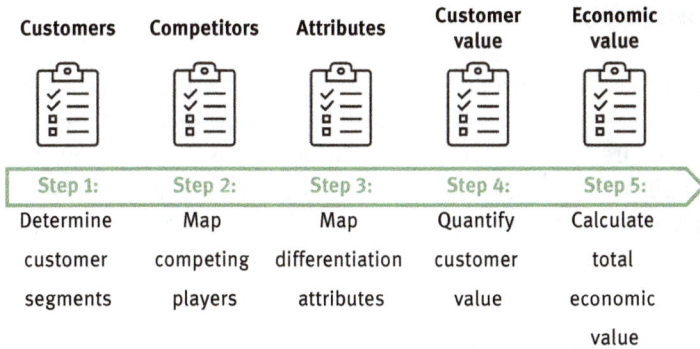

Figure 2.2: Steps in the VTC Analysis.

segment. In Chapter 5, I explain in more detail how one can map out how customers vary with respect to the attributes they want.

Step 2: Map Competing Players

The next step in the VTC analysis is to compare your product against the best *alternative* the customer segment can choose. Try to be as specific as possible. Ask what customers would have bought *if your product had not been on the market*. This is the "next best alternative." Such a comparison is essential for that value-based pricing to work. This also means that the method works best if there are real alternatives in the market. And it almost always does.

Step 3: Map Differentiation Attributes

Then you need to map out which attributes *differentiate* your product from the best alternative. You do this by looking at the different product attributes and deciding where you are better, but also where you are worse than the competition. Remember that these attributes must be *visible*, *clear*, and *important* to the customer when making their purchasing decisions.

It can be difficult for customers to specify which attributes are most important to them. They may just feel what is right or know what they do not want. The work to identify attributes is thus important and defines the guidelines for what is analyzed and quantified later. Often the sellers are the closest to having this knowledge as they are in contact with customers daily. Sellers can compare across customer segments and product types and will, in many cases, be better placed to define the essential attributes. Not least, sellers know what qualities customers are willing to sacrifice to buy a product or service.

Step 4: Quantify Customer Value

The next point, and perhaps the most difficult, is *quantifying* the practical value the customer segment puts on the differentiation attributes. Remember, this includes only the attributes that are different (both better and worse). I will go through in detail how this quantification is done in the conjoint analysis in Chapter 3. It is also possible to use qualitative customer interviews, although this is a far more subjective and therefore more unreliable method.

In the corporate market, examples of such quantification include:
- changes in wage costs and compensation – measured in $
- productivity change – measured in time
- user training costs – measured in $
- maintenance costs – measured in $
- duration – measured in $
- reliability and downtime – measured in $
- installation costs – measured in $
- employment costs, severance packages – measured in $
- raw material costs – measured in $
- production costs – measured in $
- access to new markets and customers – measured in $

In the consumer market there is also a whole range of practical ways to quantify attributes. For example, a Wi-Fi provider can be assessed based on the following attributes:
- purchasing costs for equipment – measured in $
- installation costs – measured in $
- training costs for use of the equipment – measured in time
- reliability and downtime for the Internet – measured in $, use of 5G as a replacement
- subscription costs – measured in $
- duration of the equipment – measured in $
- speed – measured in time
- portability – measured in $, if you can use the Internet in several places, e.g., a cabin
- coverage – measured in $, use of 5G as a replacement
- product packages – measured in $, how much the price is affected by several services from the same supplier

The goal of Step 4 is thus to quantify the attributes that set us apart from the competing alternatives.

Step 5: Calculate Total Economic Value

The last step in the VTC analysis is to sum up the numbers and calculate the total economic value for the customers. It is easy to take a wrong step and think that this is the market value of the product. It is not. These calculations define the maximum price you can get in the market, given a normal competitive situation. If your competitor has completely irrational prices, or suddenly dumps their prices, your price calculations must take this into consideration. However, before you follow and dump the prices yourself, read Chapter 6 on price wars so you do not fall into a price war trap.

Mistakes Made in Value-Based Pricing

An entrepreneur or startup company probably often thinks that their product is fantastic for all types of customers. They often have difficulties understanding the purpose of prioritizing specific customer segments. It is important to emphasize that defining a specific target group does not mean that the other customer groups are not wanted. However, it is often financially impossible for a small business to communicate and serve many customer segments at the same time. Prioritization in terms of targeting customer groups simply means that you start with the customers you are most likely to succeed with.

A common mistake that is made with value-based pricing is that one includes all the functions of a product [14]. This is practically impossible as even very a simple product can have dozens of functions. Just think of cellphones. They vary in terms of brand, screen size, performance, storage, camera function, color, technology, accessories, and so on. A proper method is to *value the attributes as being different, visible, distinct, and important for the customer segment.*

A second mistake that is made is to expect the customer's perception of value to be the same as that of the manufacturer [15]. The producers, market operators, and sellers of a product have in-depth knowledge of how the product works, and how it differs from competing products. The customers do not necessarily have the same knowledge. Their perceived value is therefore often below the total economic value as they do not know all the product attributes.

Value-based pricing is not a guarantee of success. It is important to be aware that the starting point is the price of the best competing alternative for customers. However, if this competitor has a completely random pricing strategy, it will also affect your market price. If they price their products far below market value, it is difficult to convince customers of the excellence and value of your products. This means that in some product categories you have intelligent competitors and can use value-based pricing. In other product categories, you may have no choice but to follow a competitor-based pricing strategy.

One challenge with value-based pricing is quantifying abstract attributes, such as status, brand value, and exclusivity. This can be coded into the conjoint analysis, but the results must be used with caution. The more abstract an attribute is, the more difficult it is to quantify it. Therefore, it is easier to use value-based pricing in the business market and in service industries [9]. A plumber can, for example, calculate how much water and electricity their heating system reduces customers' costs. The more specific the attributes, the easier it is to calculate the monetary value of the differentiation values.

Practical Example of VTC Analysis

In the following section, I will show a practical example of a VTC analysis using numbers.

The numbers used are taken from an example of fans that are exemplified in the next chapter of the book. There you will see the actual calculation of the value of the attributes of a fan and how the target group is identified. The fans vary in area of use (table fan/pedestal fan/ceiling fan), control (manual/remote control), color (black/white), and price ($39.90/$45.00/$55.00).

In the example here, we use the figures for a traditional customer segment that is concerned with comfort. Mostly white fans are relevant for these customers. Because they like to have the fan both inside and outside on hot days, they prefer pedestal fans. One of the biggest competitors on the market, Home Depot, sells beautiful black pedestal fans for $39.99. However, these do not have a remote control, but Home Depot believes that the beautiful black color compensates for this. Also, their fans use less power, estimated at $1 per season.

The VTC analysis for the fans is illustrated graphically in Figure 2.3. In the next chapter, we have calculated the value of the various attributes. This is called the "differentiation value." The differentiation value for remote control is $1.08 and for color $3.56, a total of $4.64. The negative differentiation value (electricity cost) is $1. Based on the analysis, the economic value for white pedestal fans for our customers, given the competitor, is $43.63. A selling price of $42.99 can therefore be a realistic alternative to signal a good deal.

Summary

This chapter has described value-based pricing and has shown a very practical example of how to implement value-based pricing. For this, the VTC analysis tool was used. Within pricing, VTC analysis stands for "value-to-customer estimation." VTC analysis ensures a comprehensive understanding of a company's pricing strategy, including how to determine the customer group, map competitors, identify unique

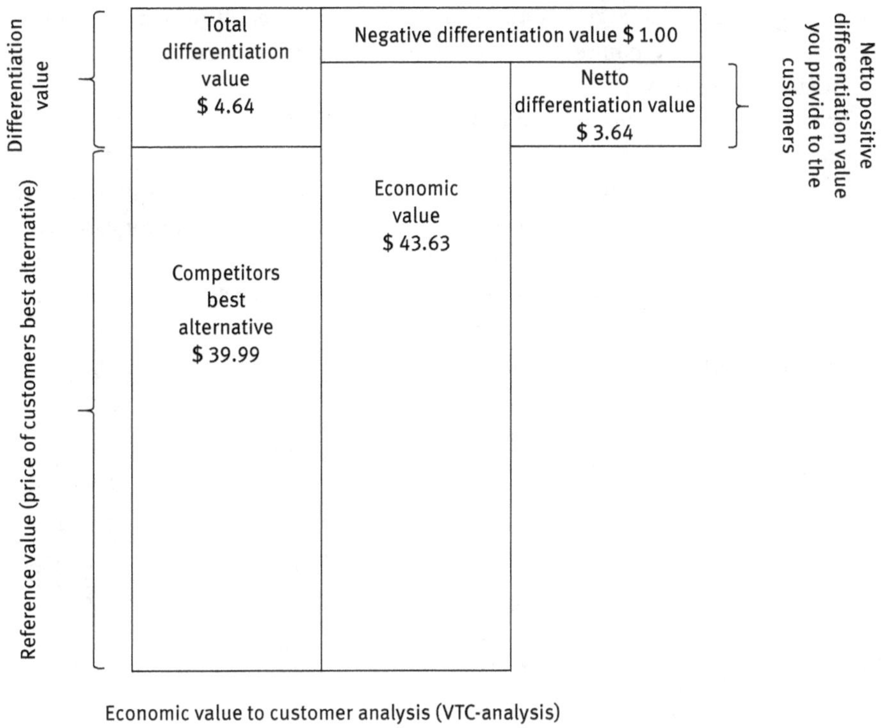

Differentiation value

Negative differentiation value $ 1.00

Total differentiation value $ 4.64

Netto differentiation value $ 3.64

Netto positive differentiation value you provide to the customers

Economic value $ 43.63

Competitors best alternative $ 39.99

Reference value (price of customers best alternative)

Economic value to customer analysis (VTC-analysis)

Figure 2.3: VTC Analysis Graphical Layout.

product attributes, and set a numerical value for these attributes. This is then estimated into a total economic value to the customer. At the end of the chapter, I discuss mistakes that are easy to make when starting with value-based pricing. As an appendix to the chapter, I have added a case demonstrating VTC analysis in practice.

Attachment: VTC Analysis for the Case "Harmony Cottage Village"

The example we are going to use is based on the "Harmony Cottage Village," where the numbers are calculated in the conjoint analysis in the next chapter. Let's say that a competitor, "Bear Cottage Village," sells cabins for $225,000. These cabins are built from log, but they only offer cabins by the water. Their price thus forms the customers' best alternative, here called the "reference value."

The cabins we offer have the following differentiation attributes – they are built from log (value $9,340) and you can get undisturbed land (value $10,899). Our customers can also get turnkey cabins, but this is the same as the competition, so there is no differentiation value. In total, our differentiation values amount to $20.239 (see Figure 2.4). "Bear Cottage Village," however, offers fiber optic Internet and TV connection, to a value of $1,990. "Harmony Cottage Village" cannot offer this.

From the figure for analysis for economic value (VTC analysis), we see that the maximum price we can charge in the market is $243,249. One strategy for setting this type of price, especially for expensive products, is to take the net differentiation value and divide this equally between buyer and seller. Such a compromise creates goodwill, and the customer gets the experience that one wants to find common values. In this case, it amounts to approximately $10,000 per party in the transaction. The sale price for a log cabin located, undisturbed, in "Harmony Cottage Village" is therefore set at $233.249.

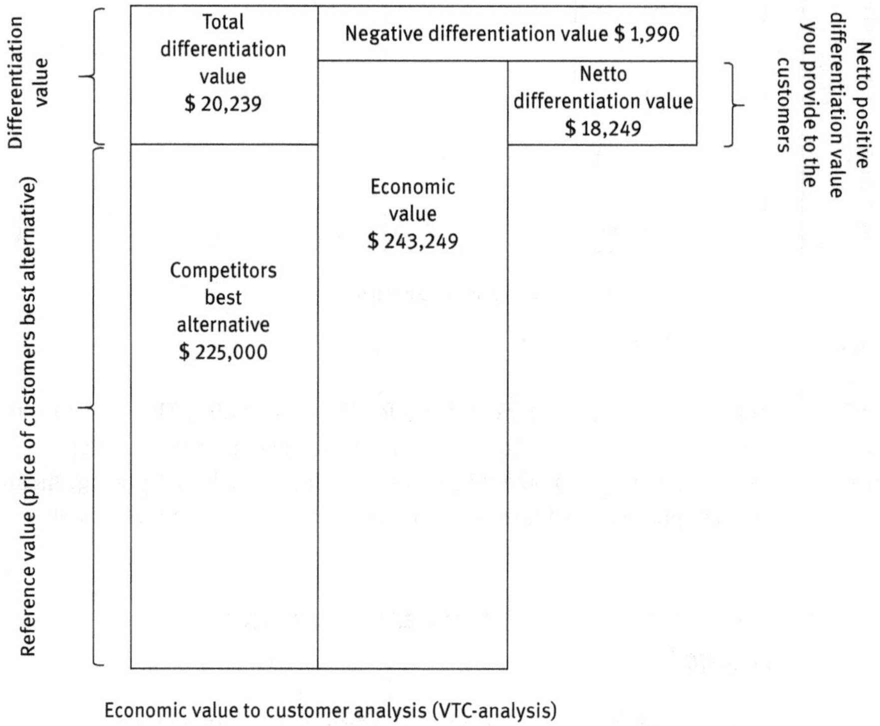

Economic value to customer analysis (VTC-analysis)

Figure 2.4: VTC Analysis for "Harmony Cottage Village".

Chapter 3
Measure Customers' Reactions to Price Changes

Introduction

Deciding on how much to raise or lower the price is a difficult decision. If you increase the price too much, the company's sales volume is reduced. If you increase the price too little, the company loses potential income. It is difficult to balance how much a price can change and obtain the desired reaction pattern among customers. Often, the flexibility and ease in setting prices up and down prevents companies from working long-term with their pricing strategy. Price adjustments are often based on gut feeling, intuition, or the marketer's experience [16]. And managers often get away with this practice, as it is difficult to verify what sales would be like if price changes were made through informed and competent decisions.

Price sensitivity measures how customers react to price changes. This way we can know how customers will react – before we have made the change itself. In this chapter, I will go through the most common ways to measure customers' price sensitivity. The chapter is divided into two main parts. In the first part, I describe the most common techniques for measuring price reactions. In part two, I present a detailed review of the Van Westendorp model and conjoint analysis. Both techniques are widely used in launching new products or for incremental (gradual) product innovations.

Measure Price Sensitivity

An important price question companies ask themselves is predicting how customers will *react* to various price changes. Price sensitivity measures customers' reactions to price levels and price changes. If customers have low price sensitivity, the price can change more without reducing sales, in contrast to customers that have high price sensitivity.

To map customers' reactions to prices, it is crucial to ask what is called "representative customers." A representative customer means that he or she is qualified to answer the questions, and must meet the following criteria:
- The customer must be real, i.e., he or she is an actual buyer of the product.
- The characteristics of the customer must represent the customer segment that the person represents.
- The customer must represent the segmented group.

https://doi.org/10.1515/9783110987102-003

Figure 3.1 shows an overview of four ways to measure price sensitivity. This discussion draws on Nagle and Müller's [4] in-depth description of these categories. These are historical data, through direct measurements, experiments, and scenarios. I explain everything in more detail below. The table further divides into two dimensions. An *uncontrolled condition* of the measurements means that it is not possible to know whether there are factors other than our price change that affect customers' purchase or their intention to buy. This can, for example, be competitors' price changes, changed wage conditions, family situation, or all kinds of external factors. The second dimension is the *controlled condition* for the measurements. This means that you know whether the purchases, or purchase intentions, are made due to the price changes. Unfortunately, such controlled conditions are tested in an artificial situation, so that a real effect on customers' decision-making cannot be guaranteed.

Conditions for the measurements

	Uncontrolled	*Controlled*
Actual purchases	Historical data	Experiments
Preferences and intentions	Direct measurement	Scenarios

Figure 3.1: Techniques for Measuring Price Sensitivity (adapted from Nagle and Müller [4]).

Historical Data

Companies hold huge amounts of data from scanning solutions in the cash registers and from online purchases. These data can be categorized and adapted to get calculations on sales within product type, product categories, geographical regions, and different time periods, as well as for different retailers, volume of sales, products sold together, and so on. Big data and techniques such as web scraping are also used more and more to catch up with the major trends in sales fluctuations in markets.

Examples of historical data:
– historical sales data
– panel data
– store scanner data

Graphic and visual solutions in Excel can present complicated sales figures in simple ways so that you get a quick overview of the sales situations. Such overview graphs will, however, never be able to isolate the specific effects of price variations. The reason is that you can never eliminate competitors' measures, customers' changing preferences, or other market changes. An overview of the sales will still be better than no use of the data.

In the following Excel figures, I have demonstrated how to make a graphical pivot table of sales figures (see Table 3.1 and Figures 3.2–3.5), in addition to color marking columns for simple illustration of sales results (see Figure 3.6).

Table 3.1: Excel Data for Pivoting – Sample Data.

Order date	Region	Sales person	Product	Numbers	Cost per unit	Total
15.01.2022	Central	Jones	Blinders	46	8,99	413,54
01.02.2022	Central	Smith	Blinders	87	15,00	1 305,00
18.02.2022	East coast	Johnson	Blinders	4	4,99	19,96
07.03.2022	West coast	Williams	Blinders	7	19,99	139,93
24.03.2022	Central	Johnsen	Colours	50	4,99	249,50
10.04.2022	Central	Andrews	Pencils	66	1,99	131,34
27.04.2022	East coast	Lopez	Penner	96	4,99	479,04
14.05.2022	Central	Jones	Pencils	53	1,29	68,37
31.05.2022	Central	Jones	Blinders	80	8,99	719,20
17.06.2022	Central	Davis	Tables	5	125,00	625,00
04.07.2022	East coast	Johnson	Colours	62	4,99	309,38
21.07.2022	Central	Wilson	Colours	55	12,49	686,95
07.08.2022	Central	Davis	Colours	42	23,95	1 005,90
24.08.2022	West coast	Williams	Tables	3	275,00	825,00
10.09.2022	Central	Jones	Pencils	7	1,29	9,03
27.09.2022	West coast	Williams	Penner	76	1,99	151,24
14.10.2022	West coast	Hill	Blinders	57	19,99	1 139,43
31.10.2022	Central	Andrews	Pencils	14	1,29	18,06
17.11.2022	Central	Johnsen	Blinders	11	4,99	54,89
04.12.2022	Central	Johnsen	Blinders	94	19,99	1 879,06
21.12.2022	Central	Andrews	Blinders	28	4,99	139,72
06.01.2023	East coast	Johnson	Pencils	95	1,99	189,05
23.01.2023	Central	Davis	Blinders	50	19,99	999,50
09.02.2023	Central	Johnsen	Pencils	36	4,99	179,64
26.02.2023	Central	Jones	Penner	27	19,99	539,73
15.03.2023	West coast	Williams	Pencils	56	2,99	167,44
01.04.2023	East coast	Johnson	Blinders	60	4,99	299,40
18.04.2023	Central	Andrews	Pencils	75	1,99	149,25
05.05.2023	Central	Johnsen	Pencils	90	4,99	449,10
22.05.2023	West coast	Dahlstrom	Pencils	32	1,99	63,68
08.06.2023	East coast	Johnson	Blinders	60	8,99	539,40
25.06.2023	Central	Wilson	Pencils	90	4,99	449,10
12.07.2023	East coast	Lopez	Blinders	29	1,99	57,71
29.07.2023	East coast	Dahlstrom	Blinders	81	19,99	1 619,19

Table 3.1 (continued)

Order date	Region	Sales person	Product	Numbers	Cost per unit	Total
15.08.2023	East coast	Johnson	Pencils	35	4,99	174,65
01.09.2023	Central	Smith	Tables	2	125,00	250,00
18.09.2023	East coast	Johnson	Colours	16	15,99	255,84
05.10.2023	Central	Wilson	Blinders	28	8,99	251,72
22.10.2023	East coast	Johnson	Penner	64	8,99	575,36
08.11.2023	East coast	Dahlstrom	Penner	15	19,99	299,85
25.11.2023	Central	Davis	Colours	96	4,99	479,04
12.12.2023	Central	Smith	Pencils	67	1,29	86,43
29.12.2023	East coast	Dahlstrom	Colours	74	15,99	1 183,26

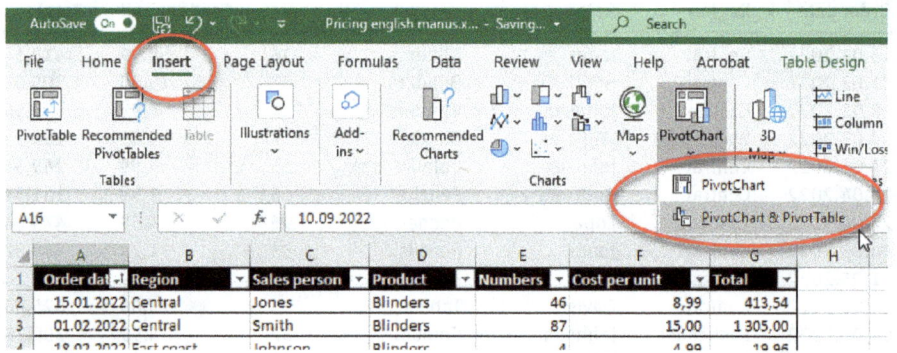

Figure 3.2: Dialog Box for Graphical Pivoting in Excel.

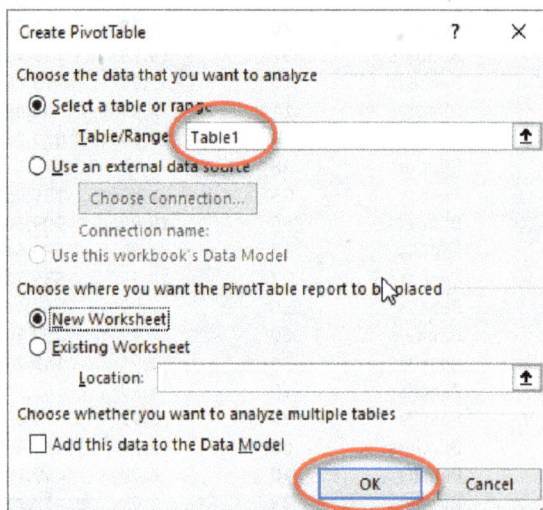

Figure 3.3: Graphical Pivoting Dialog Box in Excel – Select Spreadsheets.

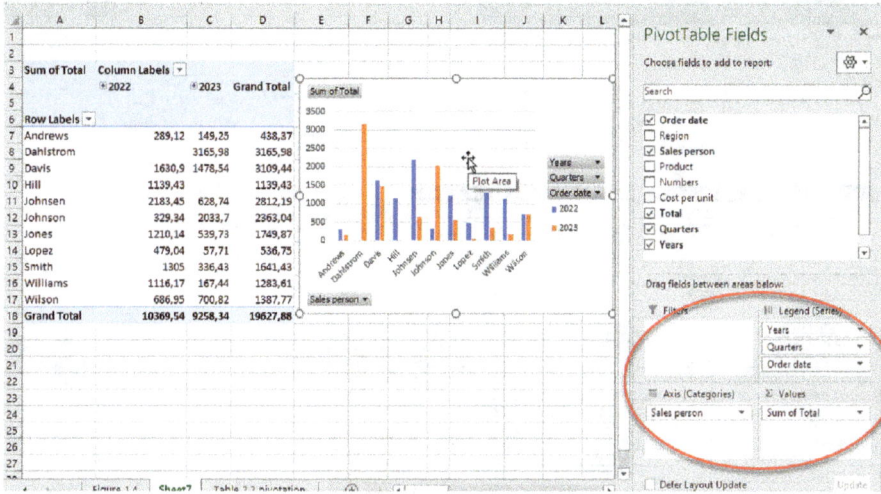

Figure 3.4: Graph of Pivoting in Excel – Total Sales per Seller per Year.

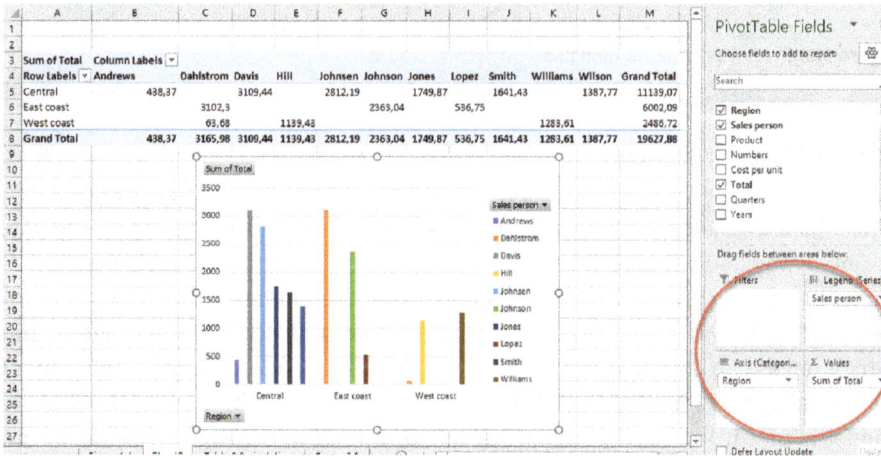

Figure 3.5: Graph of Pivoting in Excel – Total Sales per Geographical Area per Seller.

The historical data can only provide sales illustrations. To include a change in sales after a change in price, the data sets must include this kind of information.

Order date	Region	Sales person	Product	Numbers	Cost per unit
15.01.2022	Central	Jones	Blinders	46	
01.02.2022	Central	Smith	Blinders	87	
18.02.2022	East coast	Johnson	Blinders	4	
07.03.2022	West coast	Williams	Blinders	7	
24.03.2022	Central	Johnsen	Colours	50	
10.04.2022	Central	Andrews	Pencils	66	
27.04.2022	East coast	Lopez	Penner	96	
14.05.2022	Central	Jones	Pencils	53	
31.05.2022	Central	Jones	Blinders	80	
17.06.2022	Central	Davis	Tables	5	125,00	625,00
04.07.2022	East coast	Johnson	Colours	62	4,99	309,38
21.07.2022	Central	Wilson	Colours	55	12,49	686,95
07.08.2022	Central	Davis	Colours	42	23,95	1 005,90
24.08.2022	West coast	Williams	Tables	3	275,00	825,00
10.09.2022	Central	Jones	Pencils	7	1,29	9,03
27.09.2022	West coast	Williams	Penner	76	1,99	151,24
14.10.2022	West coast	Hill	Blinders	57	19,99	1 139,43
31.10.2022	Central	Andrews	Pencils	14	1,29	18,06
17.11.2022	Central	Johnsen	Blinders	11	4,99	54,89
04.12.2022	Central	Johnsen	Blinders	94	19,99	1 879,06
21.12.2022	Central	Andrews	Blinders	28	4,99	139,72
06.01.2023	East coast	Johnson	Pencils	95	1,99	189,05
23.01.2023	Central	Davis	Blinders	50	13,99	999,50
09.02.2023	Central	Johnsen	Pencils	36	4,99	179,64

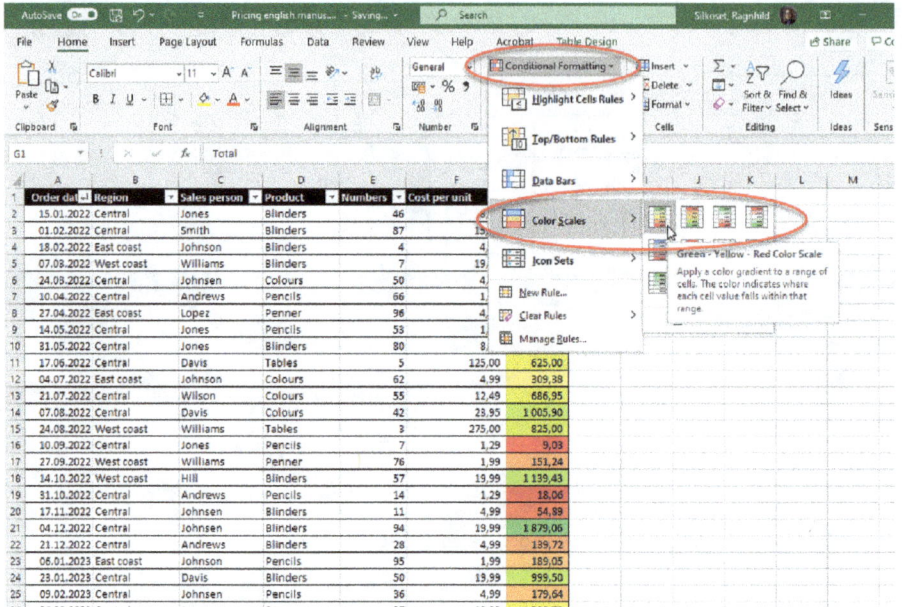

Figure 3.6: Excel – Color Mark Columns.

Direct Measurements

Direct measurements are based on an assessment of customers' willingness to pay. A simple way to determine the price of products and services is through direct questions, i.e., asking a representative customer what the minimum and maximum prices are that they are willing to pay. This gives an indication of the range within which prices can vary and is known as the "Van Westendorp model." This way of determining price is simple and easy to implement [6]. The drawback with the model is that it forces respondents to relate themselves to a specific price, even though this might not necessarily be right for them. A more indirect way to determine the price is to ask them what price they think is so reasonable that they would be unsure of the quality of the product, as well as what price they think would make a good buy. The results are plotted in a graph and show the range for an acceptable price level. At the end of the chapter, there is a more practical demonstration of the Van Westendorp model.

Examples of direct measurements:
- direct questions (*Van Westendorp model*)
- purchase response survey
- in-depth interviews

Experiment

The extensive use of online stores provides opportunities to run price experiments by manipulating prices for a period and comparing the effects of previous periods. The difficulty here is that you cannot know whether the changes in sales are due to price changes only, or whether there are other external factors that also affect the market. To control for the latter, a laboratory experiment ensures that all external factors are stable. The disadvantage is that the setting is artificial and therefore does not necessarily reflect true behavior. If one has more than one outlet, it can be a good technique to change the prices in some of them, while they are held steady in the others. This allows for a better test of whether the sales variation is due only to the price change or other external factors.

Examples of experiments:
- in-store experiments
- laboratory-purchase experiments

Scenarios

In scenarios, different combinations of product alternatives are first created and presented to selected customers. Customers are then asked to rank the options regarding attractiveness and purchase probability. The scenario methods provide a good and detailed basis for analyzing various price effects on decisions. Sequential preferences are a technique where the customer is asked to choose between pairs of options where prices vary. Selection analysis (trade-off) gives the respondents a set of product descriptions and price variations, and the respondents must then either choose between the most important attributes or make a ranking of different combinations of alternatives. The latter is called "conjoint analysis" and is described in detail later in the chapter.

Simulated-purchase experiments are artificial shops where selected customers go in and select products. Thus, they can vary in location, price, selection, and alternative products.

Examples of scenarios:
- choice analysis (conjoint analysis)
- simulated-purchase experiments

In the next section, I show a practical example of how to run a conjoint analysis. All calculations are done using an Excel spreadsheet.

The Van Westendorp Model for Price Calculations

The Van Westendorp model was introduced in 1976 by the Dutch economist Peter Van Westendorp [17]. In the model, the respondent (customer) is asked to assess the value of different price points. A prerequisite for the model is thus that respondents can associate perceived value to price. It is important to be aware that the results may be misleading if this assumption is violated. On the other hand, the Van Westendorp method is cheap and easy to use, and it provides a clear graphical visualization that shows the demand in various price ranges.

In the Van Westendorp model, the respondent must consider four factors around the price of a product or service:

1. too expensive
2. too cheap
3. expensive
4. cheap

The Van Westendorp method is best fitted early in the product development process when the customer has not yet developed a completely clear idea about exact prices [18]. One disadvantage here is that you may end up with very large price intervals, which could make it difficult to implement the results. In addition, the results can be quite unstable. One way of overcoming this is for the company to first set the price range to be assessed, and then ask the respondent to define its acceptable prices within the specific price range. This prevents irrelevant alternatives.

Steps in the Development and Implementation of the Van Westendorp Model

The Van Westendorp model is useful due to its ease of use (see Figure 3.7). It provides insight into price ranges within which the company can work. The model can, however, be used advantageously in combination with other techniques to measure price sensitivity. A *combination* of sales data and data where one captures reflections on customers' buying process will provide useful additional information. An example of the latter is conjoint analysis, which is described in this chapter.

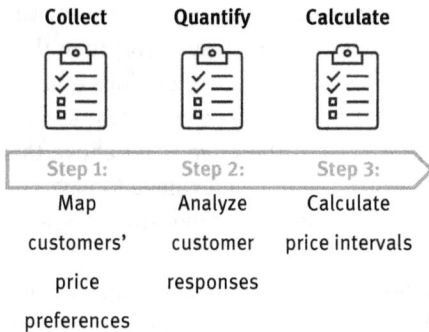

Figure 3.7: Steps in the Van-Westendorp Model.

Step 1: Map Customers' Price Preferences

To map customers' price preferences, the Van Westendorp model uses four simple questions. These are:
1. At what price is this product too expensive? (too expensive)
2. What price would be so low that you begin to ask questions about the quality of this product? (too cheap)
3. At what price does this product start to seem expensive? (expensive)
4. At what price do you think this product is starting to become a bargain – good value for money? (cheap)

As with any data collection, it is important to have representative customers who respond to the survey. This is explained in more detail elsewhere in the book.

Step 2: Analyze Customer Responses

In the graph in Figure 3.8, the x-axis represents the price ranges, while the y-axis represents the number of respondents in percent. As the price increases, the number of respondents that perceive the product as being too cheap or a good purchase is reduced. At the same time, the number of people who perceive the product as being too expensive or quite expensive is increasing. This creates three crossing points that provide important information about ideal price ranges:
1. the point of marginally too cheap
2. the point of marginally too expensive
3. optimal price point

The point of marginally too cheap marks the lowest recommended price for the product. In our graph this is approximately $226. If the price is set lower than this, the buyers will think that the product is too cheap and therefore of dubious quality. In the opposite case, the point of marginally expensive marks the highest acceptable price in the market. This is approximately $280. If the price is set above this limit, customers will not think the product is worth the price they have to pay. The optimal price point is where expensive and cheap cross each other. In our graph, this is approximately $250.

Such an interpretation, however, requires there to be a lower limit for questionable quality. There is a whole range of products where you buy more and more the cheaper the product, for example small items in bulk. In such cases, the model provides less valuable information. Another challenge with this type of question is, of course, that the respondents can deliberately answer that they want an unnatural low price.

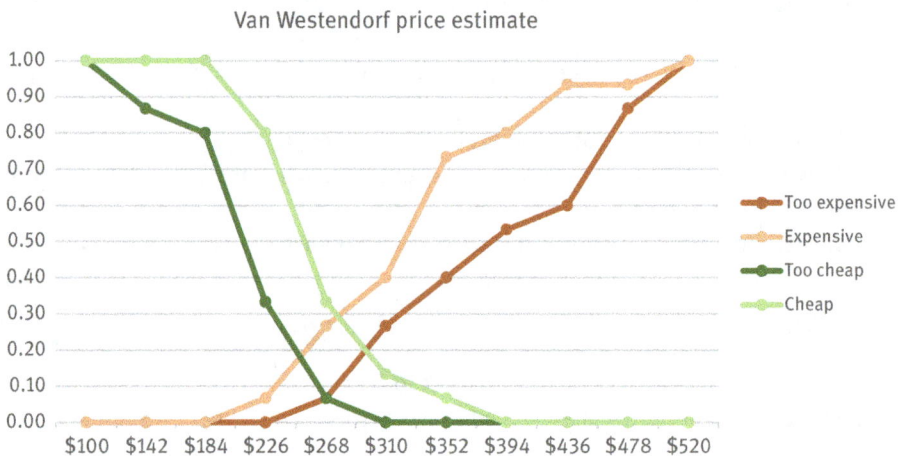

Figure 3.8: From Westendorp Figure.

Step 3: Calculate Price Ranges

The interval between marginally cheap and marginally expensive is the price range within which prices can be adjusted. In theory, the cutoff point is the optimal price point, the price at which customers report the optimal price, i.e., where as many people as possible are satisfied with the price.

Because the model requires customers to know the value of the product, the Van Westendorp model is particularly useful in the business market, where customers have in-depth knowledge of the value of the products and services they purchase. The method is less effective in the consumer goods market as customers do not necessarily know the value of a product. It is therefore important to include extensive product information when the survey is conducted on consumers. This will ensure a better quality of answers.

It is important to be aware that the optimal price point for a product is not necessarily the optimal price for the company. The Van Westendorp model does not consider the company's fixed and variable costs. Calculations of profitability analysis can therefore show a different optimal price.

The model gives no regard to competitors' reactions [18]. The model is therefore most stable for new products where there are few competitors. Of course, this happens very rarely. It is therefore recommended that the Van Westendorp model is used in combination with the other techniques described in this chapter.

Conjoint Price Analysis

The informational value of a conjoint analysis comes from the fact that it analyzes the price sensitivity of the actual attributes of a product. A conjoint analysis identifies, combines, quantifies, and calculates the effect of these product attributes. This analysis can be done quite advanced with specialized statistical analysis tools and various analysis models. However, this does not fit the target audience of this book. In the appendix to this chapter, I have chosen to show the procedure and the analysis using Excel. A more detailed explanation of this analysis is included.

Steps in the Development and Implementation of Conjoint Analysis

I have chosen to divide the conjoint analysis into four steps to demonstrate how to conduct the analysis with the purpose of identifying the value of various attributes of a product (see Figure 3.9): Step 1: Identify customer preferences; Step 2: Develop product profiles; Step 3: Analyze customer compromises; and Step 4: Calculate the economic effect.

A conjoint analysis involves data collection among customers. Therefore, the customer sample must consist of people interested in buying the product. If not, the results of the analysis have no value. It is therefore important to be sure that the customers one asks represent real buyers of the product. Earlier in the book, we emphasized that the selected customers must be qualified to answer the questions.

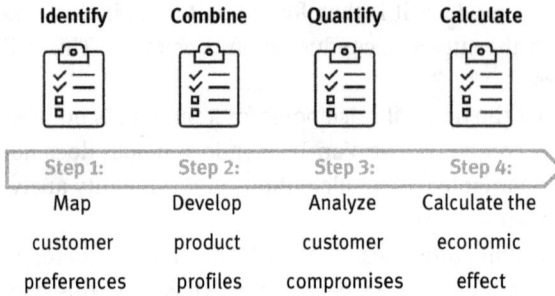

Figure 3.9: Steps in the Conjoint Analysis to Map Customers' Willingness to Pay for Product Attributes.

Step 1: Map Customer Preferences

All products and services consist of a combination of different attributes. Let's take something as basic as a fan.

Attribute 1: Application of use
Level 1: Table fan
Level 2: Pedestal fan
Level 3. Ceiling fan
Attribute 2: Control
Level 1: Manual
Level 2: Remote
Attribute 3: Color
Level 1: White
Level 2: Black
Attribute 4: Price
Level 1: $ 39.90
Level 2: $ 45.00
Level 3: $ 55.00

Figure 3.10: Attributes of a Fan. Picture from https://www.lasko.com/products/performance-table-fan-black-d12525/ 07 March 2022.

In Figure 3.10 we have defined fans as follows:
- **The main attributes** that affect the purchase of a fan are: 1. application of use; 2. control; 3. color; and 4. price.
- All of the attributes have different **levels,** referred to as "election criteria," where customers must make choices. They cannot have more than one of these election criteria at the same time.
- Combinations of the choice criteria constitute different **product profiles** for fans.

The example shows that all the products consisting of one combination of attributes together constitute the product profile. In our example, we could have combined all the attributes and all the levels and created 36 different product variants (3 applications × 2 controls × 2 colors × 3 prices).

If you ask your customers whether they want to have a fan with or without remote control, most of them will answer with remote control as it makes it easier to use the fan. Customers' answers, however, are not always based on their real needs or reflect what they would purchase. Others may respond based on what they assume the signal effect the use entails. This is particularly evident when you ask about more sensitive attributes, such as exclusive design or status. In addition, it can be difficult for customers to describe with words what they prefer when making product choices. Many products are bought unconsciously, e.g., consumables such as soap and toothpaste, while others have a whole range of different assessment situations where one carefully weighs from time to time, such as buying a sofa.

The first step in conjoint analysis is thus spending time on carefully identifying what attributes customers are considering when they buy products in the product category. These attributes can be objective, as we saw in the example with the fan. But they can also be subjective, such as how the design of a piece of furniture fits into the buyer's interior in general. Observation of purchases, interviews, and focus groups help to uncover the attributes that are important to the target group.

The attributes included in the analysis must be visible, clear, and important to the customer when they make their purchasing decisions. The purpose of conjoint analysis is thus to estimate optimal product variants for the various customer segments so that the probability of purchase increases.

Step 2: Develop Product Profiles

In the fan example, we see that the combination of product attributes and levels gives 36 different product variants. It is easy to understand that this many varieties is not appropriate. Fewer choices will lead to customers getting a "good enough" alternative and being satisfied with their choice. In addition, some options are unrealistic: for example, those that stand out with the best quality, highest performance, and lowest price. In other words, we need to identify the most relevant combination of attributes that fit the customer segment. The method explained here is based on what is called "fractional-factorial design" in conjoint analysis. This means that some product combinations have been selected for further analysis.

By setting up the alternatives, we get an overview as shown in Table 3.2. Each row (horizontal) represents the product profile, while the columns (vertical) represent specific levels within their attributes.

Table 3.2: Example of Fan Profiles.

Profile	Table fan	Pedestal fan	Ceiling fan	Manual	Remote	White	Black	$39.90	$45.00	$55.00
1	1	0	0	1	0	0	1	1	0	0
2	0	1	0	0	1	0	1	0	0	1
3	1	0	0	1	0	1	0	0	0	1
. . .										

Profile 1 is a manual table fan in the color black for $39.90. Profile 2 is a black pedestal fan with remote control for $55. Profile 3 is a manual white pedestal fan for $55. It is important to remember that the products can have only one level of attributes. As an example: a fan is either black or white.

Before we can analyze the data, there is an important next step, which in technical language is called "multicollinearity." This sounds harder than it is. In practice, this means that the data set must remove "obviousness." If the fan is white (marked with 1), we know that it is not black. And when the fan is not white (marked with 0), we know that it is black. In other words, whether the fan is white or not, we do not need to discuss the color black. This seems trivial, but it is important when we continue with the statistical analysis. It prevents biased results in our analysis. Therefore, we correct the data set by removing one of the columns at each of the attribute levels. The new data sheet looks like Table 3.3. Note too that we have added one column, which is called "assessment." We will need this shortly.

Table 3.3: Excel Spreadsheets Where One Level per Attribute Is Removed.

Profile	Table fan	Pedestal fan	Manual	White	$39.90	$45.00
1	1	0	1	0	1	0
2	0	1	0	0	0	0
3	1	0	1	1	0	0
. . .						

In our data set, we thus remove the following columns:
-   ceiling fan was removed from the application attribute
-   remote control was removed from the control attribute
-   black was removed from the color attribute
-   $55 was removed from the price attribute

Note too that we *have not lost any information* from the data set by removing these columns. This data set will be used further in the next step in the conjoint analysis.

Step 3: Analyze Customer Compromises

There are many ways to run a data collection for conjoint analysis. The positive thing is that it is easy to collect this type of data manually. There are also free online tools, such as Forms in Microsoft Office 360 and www.surveymonkey.com. Many online data collection tools with payment solutions provide conjoint solutions. One of the most common is Qualtrics.com.

When you set up the data collection, you must start with creating a range of different cards with different product combinations. An example of such a card for product packages 1 and 2 for our fan example would be the following (profile 1 is a manual table fan in the color black; see Figure 3.11). The next step is to decide who should respond to the survey. Here it is very important not to make mistakes. Those who respond, i.e., the respondents, must be representative of the target group. Put another way: Those who are asked to respond must be relevant customers. If you ask your family or friends on Facebook, you can run the risk that their answers will satisfy you, or that they are never going to buy a fan at all. Then the answers have little worth. In addition, you must think about whether you want to expand the market, meaning that you add potential customers you do not serve today.

Alternative 1	Alternative 2
Table fan	Pedestal fan
Black color	Black color
Manual control	Remote control
$39.90	$55.00

Figure 3.11: Examples of Product Sheets for Conjoint Analysis.

A common question is how many customers you need to ask. A rule of thumb is that you should have a minimum of 10 customers for each of the attributes you use in the product profiles. In the fan example, we have four attributes (type, color, control and price). This will be 4 × 10 = 40 respondents. From a statistical standpoint, it is recommended to have at least 200 respondents. In practice, this can be difficult for many small businesses, but remember that the fewer the respondents, the more unstable and inaccurate the statistical results. This means that if you have few respondents, it increases the chance of the statistical results giving wrong recommendations. After the respondents have been identified, the next step is to run the data collection. There are several ways to do this. One can ask respondents to put cards in rank order, where the most attractive combination is added at the top, etc. The order is noted by the person that carries out the survey, and the ranking is added to the data sheet in Excel. Another way is to ask respondents to give a score on how attractive they think the option is. Here you can select a scale, for example from 1 to 5, where 1 is very unattractive, 2 is unattractive, 3 is neutral, 4 is attractive, and 5 is very attractive. One can also ask them to specify the probability in percent of them wanting to buy the product on the card. For the analysis that is used in this book, it is important that respondents select their choice from one *scale*, which will give three or more alternative answers. This is called a "continuous variable." I will return to this in the analysis section.

To obtain additional knowledge about who your customers are, is it also expedient and wise to gather more data about them. In this way, you can later identify who the most attractive customers are. Examples include age, gender, income, interests, and so on. This section is, however, outside the scope of this book but is well described in many method books in economics and administrative sciences [19]. Conjoint analysis can be performed with specially developed analysis tools, with standard statistical tools, such as SPSS, R or SAS, JMP, or Excel, as shown in this book.

Step 4: Calculate the Economic Effect

This way of conducting conjoint analysis gives us the opportunity to estimate the effect of different combinations of levels on attributes.

To calculate the relative importance of the attributes in the fan example we use the number analysis from the previous step in the following way. "Utility" here is a measure of change in customer ranking.

The utility numbers in the equation correspond to what we call "unstandard beta coefficients" from the regression analysis (see the appendix for the Excel calculations). The equation shows that the price is the most important attribute when customers are considering a fan (37 percent). Then comes the color (33 percent), followed by the type of fan (27 percent). The function of the fan, i.e., whether it is manual or has a remote control, has little effect on the choice (9 percent).

Application of use	Table	1.3			
	Pedestal	2.0	$\rightarrow$	$2.0 - 0 = 2.0$	$2.0/7.4 \times 100 = 27\%$
	Ceiling	0			
Control	Manual	−0.7	$\rightarrow$	$-0.7 - 0 = -0.7$	$0.7^1/7.4 \times 100 = 9\%$
	Remote	0			
Color	White	2.0	$\rightarrow$	$2.0 - 0 = 2.0$	$2.0/7.4 \times 100 = 33\%$
	Black	0			
Price	$39.90	2.7			
	$45.00	1.7	$\rightarrow$	$2.7 - 0 = 2.7$	$2.7/7.4 \times 100 = 37\%$
	$55.00	0			

Benefit in total:
$2.0 + 0.7^1 + 2.0 + 2.7 = 7.4$

[1]We use absolute values to calculate the ratio of benefit in total.

Formula for the Importance of the Attributes

It is often best to report such numbers through illustrations. In Figure 3.12 we illustrate the importance of the attributes and in Figure 3.13 the importance of the levels of the attributes.

We already have a lot of information about which attributes the customer prefers in their choices. The next thing we can do is calculate the optimal fan! We do this by putting the numbers into an equation. b_0 is the constant term from the analysis and describes the attractiveness of the fans before considering the four aforementioned attributes. b_i is the regression coefficients. X_i is the attributes.

$$\text{Choice} = b_0 + b_1 X_1 + b_2 X_2 + b_3 X_3 + b_4 X_4$$

$$\text{Option} = b_0 + b_{1(\text{fan type})} + b_{2(\text{function})} + b_{3(\text{color})} + b_{4(\text{price})}$$

$$\text{Best choice} = 1.7 + 2\,(\text{pedestal fan}) + 0\,(\text{remote control})$$

$$+ 2\,(\text{white}) + 2.7\,(\$\,39.90) = 8.4$$

$$\text{Worst choice} = 1.7 + 0\,(\text{ceiling fan}) + (-0.7)\,(\text{manual})$$

$$+ 0\,(\text{black}) + 0\,(\$\,55) = 1$$

The most preferred fan is a white pedestal fan with remote control at £39.90. This gets a utility score of 8.4. The worst combination of attributes is a black, manual ceiling fan for $55. This gets a utility score of 1.

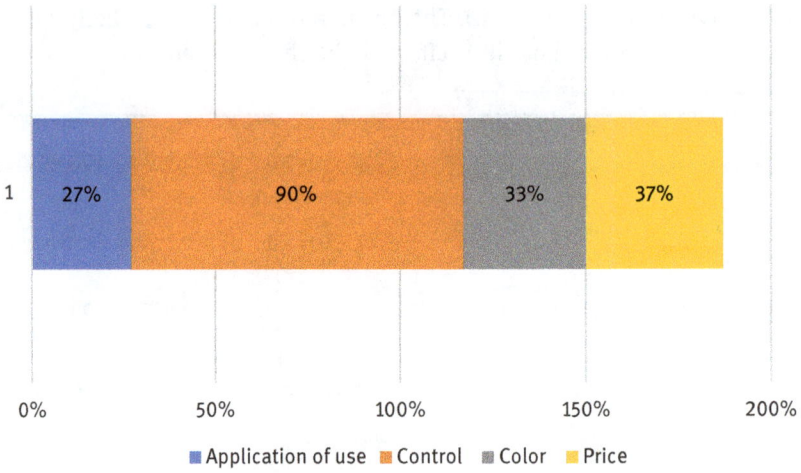

Figure 3.12: Illustration of the Importance of the Attributes of the Fan.

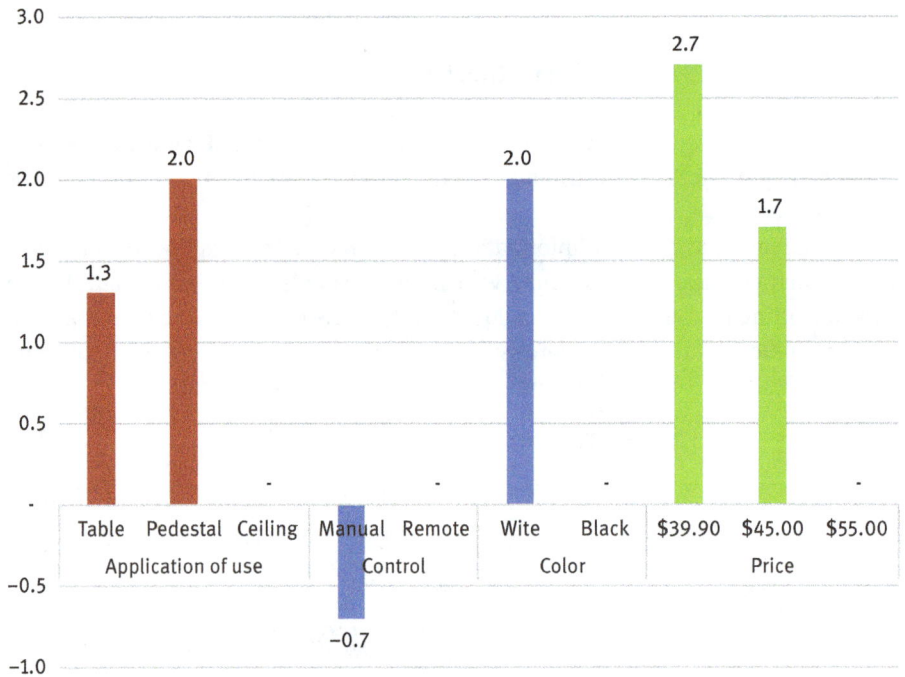

Figure 3.13: Illustration of the Importance of the Levels of the Attributes of the Fan.

Simulate Sensitivity – Utility

We can also simulate sensitivity analysis. The sensitivity analysis tells us how much we can improve (or worsen) the preferences of a product when we change one attribute while the other attributes are kept stable. Remember that we do not consider the competitors' reactions here.

Let us say that we want to simulate changes on the *table fan*, which has a utility score of 1.3. When we choose the color white, the utility score is 3.3 (1.3 + 2.0), compared to the utility score for the color black of 1.3 (1.3 + 0). When we change to the price of $39.90 the new score is 4.0 (1.3 + 2.7). For a price of $45, the utility score is 3 (1.3 + 1.7), while for a price of $55, the utility score is 1.3 (1.3 + 0).

This many numbers are better explained in a graphic illustration (see Figure 3.14).

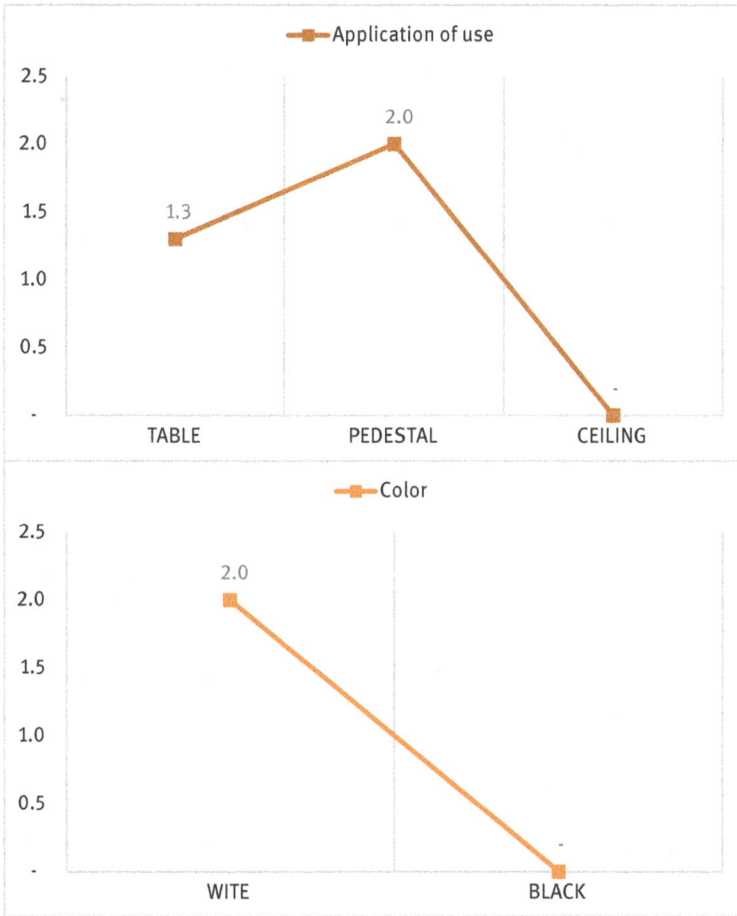

Figure 3.14: Simulation of Sensitivity for Table Fan.

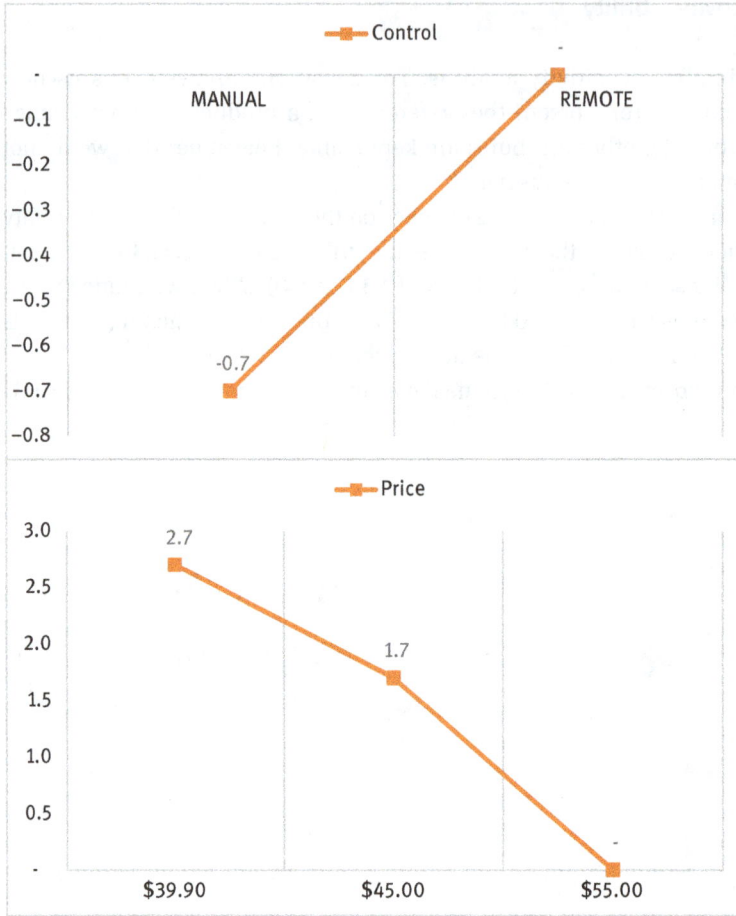

Figure 3.14 (continued)

Price Sensitivity

We can calculate the price sensitivity of each of the attributes based on the numbers we have. We do this by first estimating the utility intervals. We start this by testing the value of fan color.

The utility interval for the fan *color* can be estimated in the following way:

1.	the utility interval for price is 1.7	$(1.7 - 0 = 1.7)$
2.	the price change is $5	$(\$50 - \$45 = \$5)$
3.	each price range is worth $2.94	$(\$5/1.7 = \$2.94)$
4.	the utility interval for color is 2.0	$(2.0 - 0 = 2.0)$
5.	**willingness to pay for color is $5.88**	**$(\$2.94 \times 2 = \$5.85)$**

Based on the calculations, we find that customers have $5.85 more in terms of willingness to pay for a fan of the color white than the color black.

The relative value calculates the willingness to pay when one *also considers the other two attributes,* fan type and function.

The relative utility interval for the fan *color* can be estimated in the following way:

6. relative utility interval in total is 3.3 $(2 + (-0.7) + 2 = 3.3)$
7. relative utility interval color is 0.6 $(2/3.3 = 0.6)$
8. **relative willingness to pay color $3.56**   **$(0.6 \times 5.88 = 3.56)$**

The relative willingness to pay for color is $3.56.

We can do the same calculation for the fan function. We first create the equation with the values for the sake of overview. And then we choose the first price range to also show that example.

The relative utility interval for the fan *function* can be estimated in the following way:

1. the useful range for price is 1 $(2.7 - 1.7 = 1)$
2. the price change is $5.1 $(\$40 - \$39.90 = \$5.1)$
3. each price range is worth $5.1 $(\$5.1/1 = \$5.1)$
4. the utility interval for function is −0.7 $(-0.7 - 0 = -0.7)$
5. **fan function is worth $−3.57**   **$(\$5.1 \times -0.7 = -3.57)$**
6. relative useful range in total is 3.3 $(2 + -0.7 + 2 = 3.3)$
7. relative utility interval function is −0.2 $(-0.7/3.3 = -0.2)$
8. **relative willingness to pay for fan function is $−1.08**   **$(-0.2 \times 51 = -1.08)$**

Based on the calculations, we find that for the attribute of a manual fan, there is $3.57 *less* willingness to pay compared to a fan with remote control. Relatively speaking, in relation to the other attributes, customers have a $1.08 less willingness to pay for a manual fan.

WARNING! This type of price sensitivity analysis can be completely misleading. The analysis assumes linear relationships on price, which is not necessarily the case. The analysis assumes good-quality data. Also, the actual setup of the data collection can lead to an artificial reaction to price. Those who respond to the ranking of the alternatives may be concerned with price based on how the survey was conducted. This does not necessarily reflect price awareness in a natural setting. In addition, the analysis estimates the attributes individually. However, they can be multiplicative. For example, that the willingness to pay increases for a well-known brand, while it is lower for an unknown brand.

Simulate Market Share

Simulation of market share is limited to the data that are investigated in the analysis. If you have forgotten important attributes or do not have the right attribute combinations, the analysis will be weakened.

Simulation of market share is based on the work of Daniel McFadden, who received the Nobel Memorial Prize in Economics in 2000 for the development of a utility formula. It has the following elements:

$$\text{Market Share} = \frac{\text{Exp}\,(c \times U_A)}{\text{Exp}\,(c \times U_A) + (c \times U_B) + (c \times U_C)}$$

U_A = the probability of choosing product A, i.e., the utility estimate
C = a confidence parameter, i.e., how confident one is on the utility estimate
Exp = The exponential function. In Excel the formula is "=EXP(Cell reference)"

The formula shows four randomly selected examples of different ways of assembling a fan based on our four attributes (Table 3.4):

Table 3.4: Four Selected Fan Models.

Product	Fan type	Function (benefit)	Color (benefit)	Price (benefit)	Sum benefit	Market share
A	Table fan (1.3)	Manual (−0.7)	White (2.0)	$39.90 (2.7)	5.3	37 %
B	Table fan (1.3)	Manual (−0.7)	Black (0)	$45.00 (1.7)	2.3	2 %
C	Pedestrian fan (2.0)	Remote (0)	White (2.0)	$45.00 (1.7)	5.7	56 %
D	Pedestrian fan (2.0)	Manual (−0.7)	White (2.0)	$55.00 (0)	3.3	5 %

We put the utility values into the formula and get the following values:

$$\frac{\text{Market Share}}{\text{Product A}} = \frac{\text{Exp}\,(5.5)}{\text{Exp}\,((5.3) + (2.3) + (5.7) + (3.3))} = \frac{200}{536} = 0.37 = 37\%$$

We see that the market share for product A is 37 percent. By doing this for all models, we can estimate the distribution in market share. These are shown in Figure 3.15. The market share for product B is 2 percent, for product C it is 56 percent, and it is 5 percent for product D.

The analysis is in accordance with the findings we have obtained previously. We saw that the most attractive were white pedestal fans with remote control for $39.90

(alternative C). Because we are not willing to sell them at that price, we have here produced a simulation with a price of $45. This has given a market share of 56 percent when compared to the other three product alternatives.

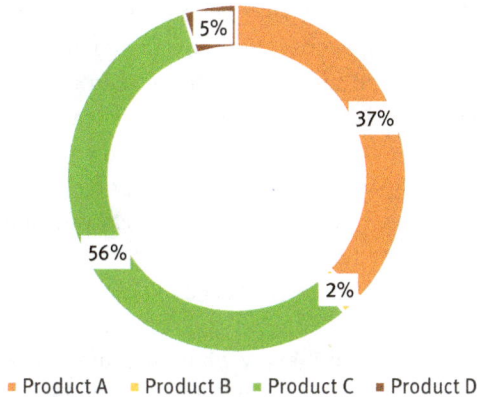

■ Product A   ■ Product B   ■ Product C   ■ Product D

Figure 3.15: Illustration of Simulated Market Share.

Summary

In this chapter, I have gone through the most common ways to measure customers' price sensitivity. The methods distinguish between prices tested in more natural situations and prices tested under more controlled conditions. Both methods have their different strengths and weaknesses. In addition, a distinction is made between measuring actual purchases and customers' intentions to buy. The chapter then described two widely used techniques for measuring price reactions, namely the Van Westendorp model and conjoint analysis. Both techniques are used in launching new products or improving product innovations. It is important to evaluate the advantages, disadvantages, weaknesses, and strengths of the models before they are used.

Case: What Should the Price Be on your New Products?

Anders M. Mamen, Lecturer, Kristiania University College

Bob works as a sales and marketing manager in a small microbrewery he has started together with some friends. Now he wonders what one 0.5-liter can of their new lager beer should cost. He has studied economics and marketing at a business school and knows that price has an impact on profitability. If the price is too high, he risks customers not buying. But if the price is too low, he ends up selling a lot of units at a low price, with poor profitability as a result. In recent months, Bob has been working on a new product. He gets positive feedback from friends, acquaintances, and potential customers. This is something they are interested in buying. When he asks what they are willing to pay for the product, he receives varying answers. The big question is: *What should a can with 0.5 liters of lager beer from our microbrewery cost?*

One thing is to look at competitors. There are many who sell beer, so he knows that they must deal with the price of competing breweries. But the new product has some attributes that competitors do not have, and he knows that they can be well paid for locally produced beer. The cost of sales and fees provides one indication of the minimum price, but since this is a new product that customers say they want, Bob thinks that he has a unique product that customers are willing to pay for.

How can Bob, with relatively simple means, find out what is the right price for the beer?

There are many different methods for finding what a product should cost. Some are good and others are less good. Here are some tips on what Bob can do.

First, he must talk to customers who buy beer and know what microbrews are. So he must ask in the right season. Customers may have a different willingness to pay on nice summer days than on a cold day in November.

Second, he should find a way to ask for what is reasonable. It is easy to get an answer that leads to the wrong conclusion. If you ask *On a scale of one to five, where one is not very probable and five is extremely likely, how likely is it that you want to buy this Pilsen in the grocery store at $4.19?*, my experience is that the answers will not make you much wiser.

It's a tool for measuring price sensitivity. The method is known as the Van Westendorp model.

What should you do if you want to use this method? First, you need to present the product in a way that customers understand. My experience from working with innovation processes is that it can be difficult to introduce new products in one simple way for customers. It is often the case that technical explanations and specifications are not important for prospective customers. What customers want to know is: *What benefits do I get by using this product?* My experience is that the best way to introduce a new product is to create one simple "ad."

Then you must ask about willingness to pay. In the Van Westendorp model, there are four questions that you must ask in a specific order:

At what price do you perceive this product as:
- so expensive that you think it's too expensive to buy?
- so cheap that you doubt the quality?
- so expensive that you think it's expensive, but you would still consider buying it?
- so cheap that you consider it a bargain?

We give the first question the name "too expensive," the second "too cheap," the third "expensive," and the fourth "cheap." Following the order of the questions is important for this to work in practice.

For a beer from a local microbrewery, $6 can be expensive, $2.50 may seem so cheap that I doubt the quality, $9 can be so expensive that I do not want to buy the product even though I really want it, while $4 can make the beer seem like a good buy.

It may be wise to give people defined prices. For one 0.5-liter can of beer from a local microbrewery one would perhaps use intervals of $0.50 or $1 between response options, but if it was a more expensive product, I would perhaps have $10 or $100 between price options. One reason for having predefined prices is that it makes it easier to analyze the results.

The next thing we need to do is to transfer the results to an analysis program, such as Microsoft Excel.

The first thing I do is to name the columns after the name of the question and rank answers in each column (regardless of the respondents) from inexpensive to expensive.

Then I delete nonsense answers: for example, those who have answered 0 for everything, and those who do not give logical answers (e.g., that "too expensive" has a lower price than "expensive").

The next thing I do is to find out what percentage have answered the various options; that is, 0 percent have said that the product is "expensive" or "too expensive" at a price of $0. Then I get the percentages of the "expensive" and "too expensive" answers in ascending order. I do this to be able to create a chart in Excel where the lines for "expensive" and "too expensive" have a rising curve.

The graphs for "cheap" and "too cheap" should have a descending curve in the chart. To achieve this, we must first do the same operation as above, and then take 100 percent and subtract the percentage that has the black price alternative (see Figure 3.16).

In a graphic representation, there will be some places where the lines intersect.
-   "Acceptable price range" is the area from where the line for "Too cheap" crosses "Expensive" to where the line for "Too expensive" crosses "Cheap."
-   The point where the lines of "Special" and "Expensive" intersect, referred to as "indifferent price," will indicate that there are just as many who think it is cheap as expensive.
-   "Optimal price" is where the lines for "Too cheap" and "Too expensive" intersect.

In this example, the recommended price range is from $4.80 to $6 (including taxes), the indifferent price is $5.50, and the optimal price is $5.80 for a 0.5-liter can of beer from the local microbrewery where Bob works.

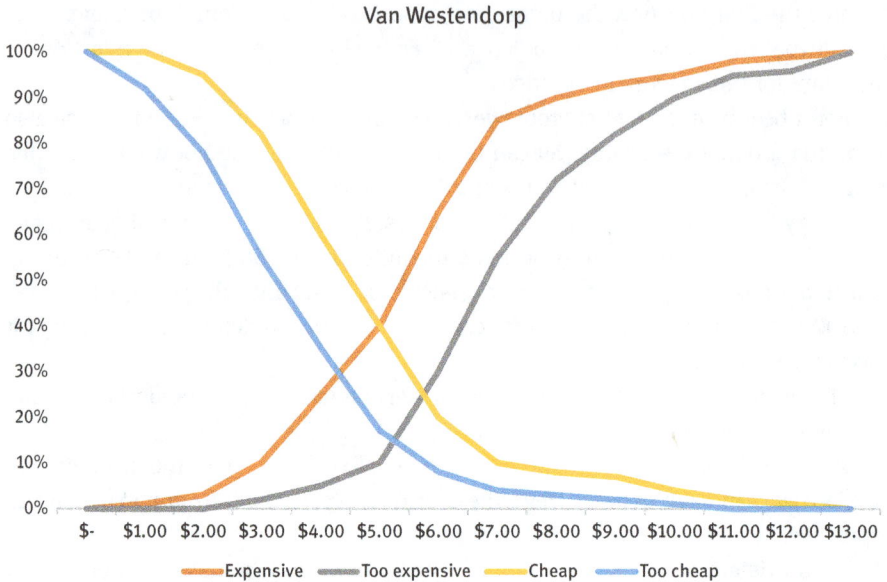

Figure 3.16: Van Westendorp Example.

Attachment: Excel for Conjoint Analysis of the Fan Example

Excel is a program that most students, companies, and entrepreneurs have access to. The choice of Excel means that I must add some pre-assumptions and make some decisions on behalf of the reader of the book. I choose a generally accepted analysis technique that fits most people, and which is based on already existing calculation functions in Excel. For those who need more advanced analysis, there are many good textbooks on conjoint analysis, in addition to market analysis agencies that also take on such assignments.

Setting Up Excel for Analysis

To use Excel, we must first *activate* the analysis function that is available for all Excel users. This feature is called "Analysis ToolPack." The procedure is as follows.

Start the Excel program. Click File> Options. Select Add-ins on the left side and then Analysis ToolPak. Then click on OK (see Figures 3.17–3.19).

In the Excel sheet, you can now click on Data on the top line (see Figure 3.20), and the analysis tool is now installed and ready for use.

There are many limitations when using Excel for this kind of analysis. One of the most common problems you encounter is that the data set cannot contain any

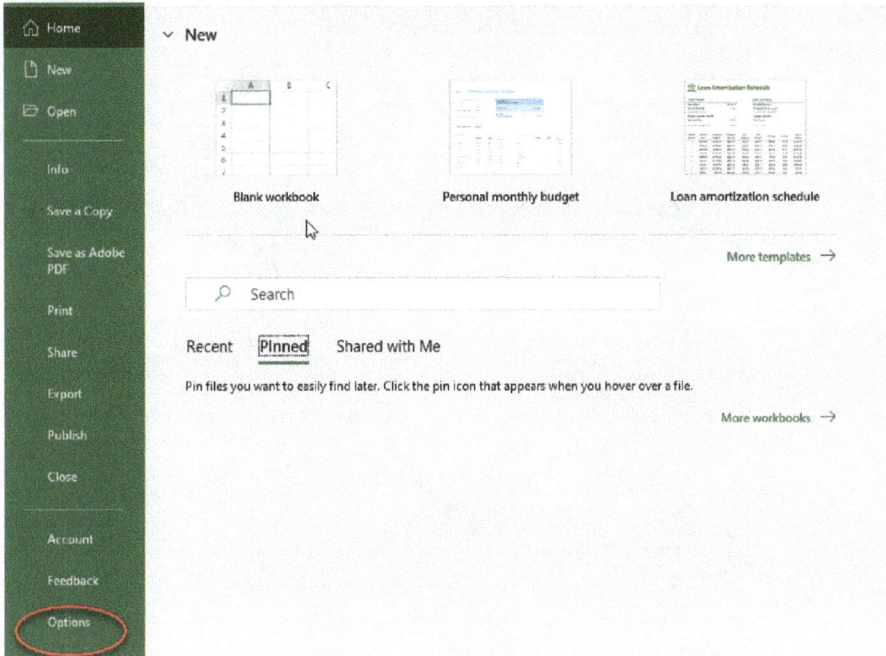

Figure 3.17: Adding Analysis Tools to Excel.

open cells (missing values), i.e., that the customer has answered "do not know" or "will not answer." Such cases must be deleted, or the missing value must be replaced. In addition, the layout of all product options should be on one side of the data sheet, while the customer's responses are on the other. We have done this in all the examples in this book, so it should be easy to follow.

In the fan example, we have now made eight options and gathered data from one customer (which is unrealistic in a real-world setting but OK for the sake of giving an example). The data set is given in Table 3.5.

We run the "fan" example in the following way. First click on Data Analysis in Excel, select Regression, then OK (see Figure 3.21).

Next, select the area in the Excel sheet where the y-variables are located. y-variables are what are called "dependent variables," i.e., the variables you want to predict with the analysis. For our example, it is the customers' preferences. These are in the range H1 to H9 in the data sheet. The x–variables are the independent variables, i.e., the variables that influence the customers' choice. In our example, this is the various product combinations we test, and in the data set, they are in columns B to G and from row 1 to 9. *Remember to exclude column A.* This is not a predictor variable but only a label of the numbering of the packages. Because each of the variables has a name at the top of the data sheet, we mark this in the Labels box. We then select OK (see Figure 3.22 for an illustration).

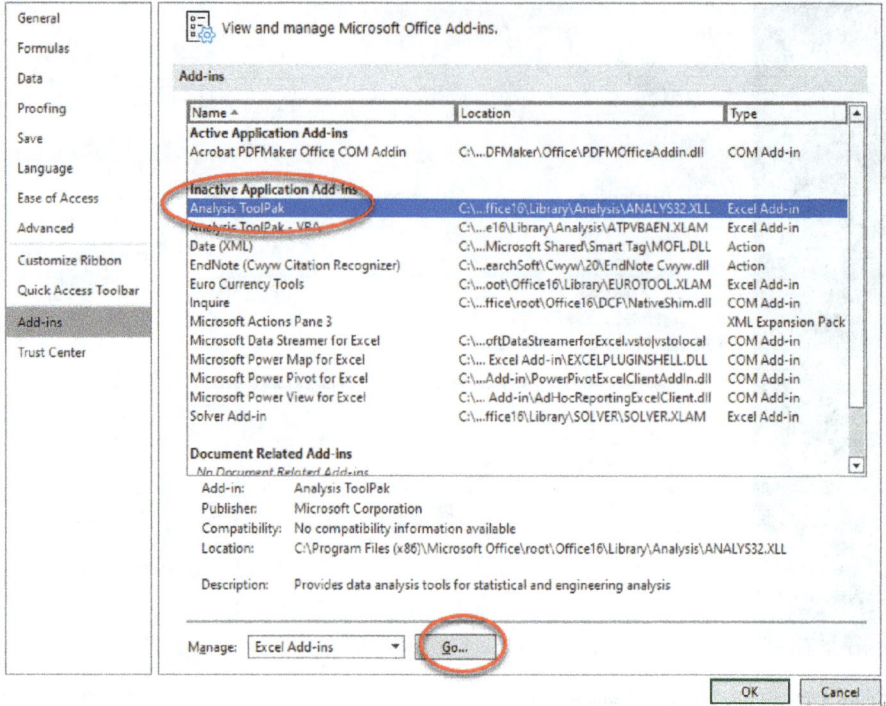

Figure 3.18: Adding Software Package to Excel.

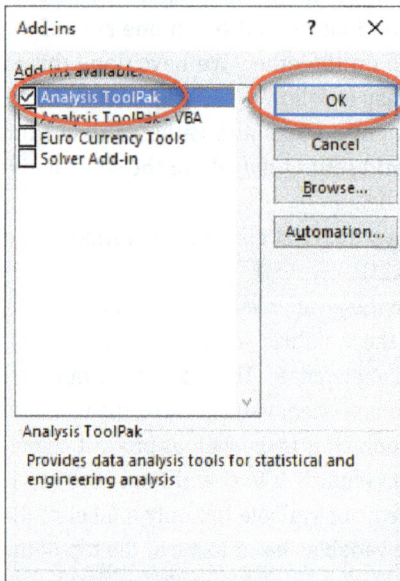

Figure 3.19: Selecting Software Package in Excel.

Table 3.5: Data Set for the Fan Example.

	A	B	C	D	E	F	G	H
1	Profile	Table	Pedestrian	Manual	White	$39	$45	Ranking
2	1	1	0	1	0	1	0	5
3	2	0	1	0	0	0	0	2
4	3	0	0	1	1	0	0	3
5	4	0	0	0	1	1	0	8
6	5	0	1	0	0	0	1	7
7	6	0	0	1	0	0	1	1
8	7	1	0	0	1	1	0	6
9	8	1	0	1	0	0	0	4

Figure 3.20: Find the Analysis Program Already Installed in Excel.

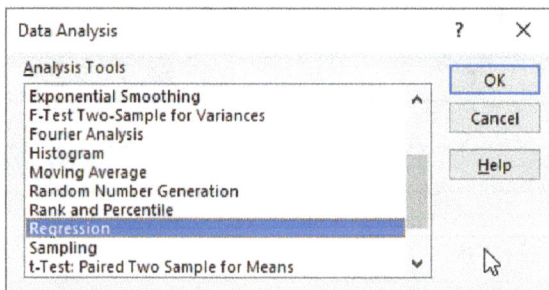

Figure 3.21: Selection of Data Analysis in Excel.

Table 3.6 shows an extract from the regression printout in Excel. I have removed some columns and reduced the number of decimals to make it more readable. There are many method books for more in-depth interpretations and explanations [19].

The first number we need to look at is R Square. This figure has values from 0 to 1. Here is the number 0.6. This means that 60 percent of the variation in customer preferences (i.e., the dependent y-variable) is explained by the attributes of the fan (i.e., the independent x–variables). In other words, 40 percent of the variation in preferences are not explained in our model.

The next numbers we are going to look at are the ones called "coefficients." The technical language name is *unstandardized beta coefficients*. These can have positive or negative values. The first coefficient, *Intercept*, with a value of 1.7, is the constant term. This is b_0. This tells us which score the respondent has on fan

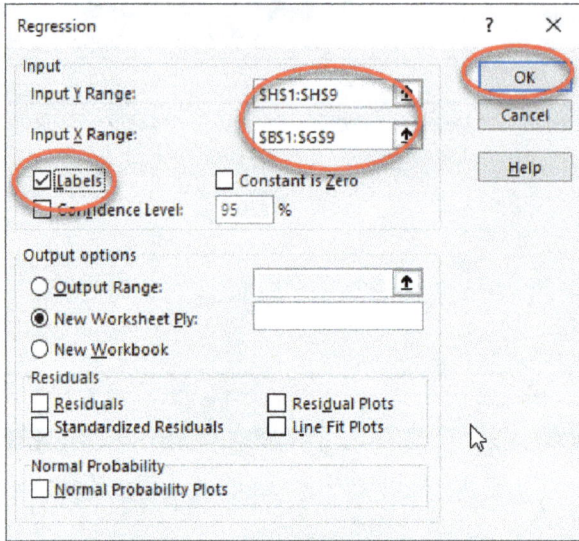

Figure 3.22: Regression Analysis Dialog Box in Excel.

Table 3.6: Results from the Regression Analysis for the Fan Example.

	A	B	C	D	E	F
1	SUMMARY OUTPUT					
2						
3	*Regression Statistics*					
4	Multiple R	0,8				
5	R Square	0,6				
6	Adjusted R Square	−1,8				
7	Standard Error	4,1				
8	Observations	8,0				
9						
10	ANOVA					
11		*df*	*SS*	*MS*	*F*	*Significance F*
12	Regression	6,0	25,3	4,2	0,3	0,9
13	Residual	1,0	16,7	6,7		
14	Total	7,0	42,0			
15						

Table 3.6 (continued)

	A	B	C	D	E	F
16		Coefficients	Standard Err	t Stat	P-value	
17	Intercept	1,7	10,7	0,2	0,9	
18	Table	1,3	4,7	0,3	0,8	
19	Pedestrian	2,0	10,0	0,2	0,9	
20	Manual	0,7	7,5	0,1	0,9	
21	White	2,0	6,5	0,3	0,8	
22	$39	2,7	5,5	0,5	0,7	
23	$45	1,7	4,7	0,4	0,8	

preferences, regardless of model, color, function, or price. The next value is *table fan*, with a beta coefficient of 1.3. This number must be interpreted against a baseline, i.e., the column we removed. Here it was the ceiling model. The number means that with a ranking from 1 to 8, the respondent reports 1.3 higher scores on the table fan compared to the ceiling model. For the *pedestal fan*, the respondent reports 2.0 higher value on his ranking compared to the ceiling model. The next number, *manual*, with −0.7, means that manual fans score 0.7 *lower* on the ranking compared to the column that was removed, i.e., remote control. In other words, customers value remote control higher than the manual fan. Then we see that the color white is to be preferred over black, with a coefficient of 2.0. For the last attribute, price, we see that a *price of $39.90* has a score that is 2.7 higher than the score for the price of $55, which is baseline. *The price of $45* has a score that is 1.7 higher than the score for the price of $55, but 1.0 lower than the score for the price of $39.90 (2.7 − 1.7 = 1.0).

Based on the analysis, we can estimate what level of attributes constitutes the optimal combinations. We take the highest value in each attribute and put them together into a product profile. In the fan example, this is a pedestal fan with remote control, the color white, and a price of $39.90. However, this solution is not necessarily strategically right. A price must also cover the costs, and $39.90 can be unrealistic even if the customers have this as their first choice.

Anyone who has worked with statistics immediately sees that none of the coefficients are significant (the *P*-value column, which should have a value of 0.05 or smaller). This is, of course, quite as expected since we have only one (!) respondent in our example. The results are therefore associated with a large degree of noise and randomness. As mentioned earlier, one should have a minimum of 200 respondents, i.e., the more the better.

The analysis technique we use is linear regression analysis. This assumes that the dependent variable is continuous, as we mentioned earlier. We solve this knowing that customers' rankings or preferences must be on a scale of three choices or more. Preferably one should have a scale of at least five choices. In our case, we used eight.

Attachment: Excel for Conjoint Analysis of the Case "Harmony Cottage Village"

In this Excel example in the book, we will develop a new cabin field, "Harmony Cottage Village," located in a valley, 1.5 hour's drive from Oslo, Norway, and a two-hour drive from the nearest ski resort, Trysil. The distance and geographic location cannot be changed. Therefore, these attributes are not included in the conjoint analysis. Instead, I have included four other attributes: the price of the ground, the location of the cottage ground, whether you want to invest your own efforts or not, and which type of cottage you prefer (see Figure 3.23).

PRODUCT TYPE:

HARMONY COTTAGE VILLAGE

ATTRIBUTES:

Price	Location	Efforts	Type

LEVELS:

$ 250 000	Water	Turnkey	Certified
$ 290 000	Undisturbed	Raw	Log

Figure 3.23: Overview of Attributes and Levels of the Product "Harmony Cottage Village".

When combining the various levels of product attributes, we end up with 16 product variants (2 price levels × 2 ground locations × 2 efforts × 2 cabin types = 16 variation options). Note that I have left out some attributes that one could expect to be important. One example is the degree of services in the form of snow removal and to-the-door delivery of groceries. These are elements that can easily be offered to the customer later through extra payment or subscription, and which do not necessarily have an impact on the cabin decision purchase.

Step 1: Map Customers' Preferences

In our Excel example from "Harmony Cottage Village," we saw that the combinations of levels and attributes led to 16 product variants. However, few cabin customers will be able to compare that many options. The next step will thus be to select the combinations that are most relevant. In Table 3.7 I have listed some suggestions for relevant alternatives. In the analysis later in the chapter, however, we will see that by collecting eight examples we can estimate the attractiveness of all 16 product alternatives.

Table 3.7: Product Options for the Case "Harmony Cottage Village".

HARMONY COTTAGE VILLAGE				
Package	**Price**	**Location**	**Efforts**	**Type**
Package 1	250000	Water	Turnkey	Certified
Package 2	290000	Water	Turnkey	Log
Package 3	250000	Undisturbed	Turnkey	Log
Package 4	290000	Undisturbed	Turnkey	Certified
Package 5	250000	Water	Raw	Log
Package 6	290000	Water	Raw	Certified
Package 7	250000	Undisturbed	Raw	Certified
Package 8	290000	Undisturbed	Raw	Log

Step 2: Develop Product Profiles

In the Excel sheet, I have chosen −1 and 1 as product selections. I have done this to show different ways to set up a data set. The data sheet will look like what follows in Table 3.8 when one has removed columns as described earlier. The empty columns from K 1 to K 15 are the customer responses we will enter later.

Step 3: Analyze Customer Compromises

In the example "Harmony Cottage Village" we have selected eight product combinations that 15 respondents were asked to rank. Table 3.9 shows the data set.

This Excel layout shows a slightly different way of performing the statistical analysis. Here, the ranking is made by the customer's value, where (1) is best. After collecting data from relevant customers, you can build a dashboard in Excel (see Figure 3.24 as an example). The figures are explained in more detail below.

Table 3.8: Eight Selected Product Combinations for "Harmony Cottage Village".

Package	Price	Location	Efforts	Type	No 1	No 2	No 3	No4	No 5	No 6	No 7	No 8	No 9	No 10	No 11	No 12	No 13	No 14	No 15
1	-1	-1	-1	-1															
2	1	-1	-1	1															
3	-1	1	-1	1															
4	1	1	1	1															
5	-1	-1	-1	-1															
6	1	-1	1	1															
7	-1	1	1	-1															
8	1	1	1	1															

Package no. 1 (first): Turnkey, environmentally certified cabin, ground by the water. $250,000.
Package no. 2 (second): Turnkey, log cabin, ground by the water. $290,000.
Package no. 8 (last): Raw building, log cabin, undisturbed ground. $290,000.

Table 3.9: Data Set for the Case "Harmony Cottage Village".

Package	Price	Location	Efforts	Type	No 1	No 2	No 3	No4	No 5	No 6	No 7	No 8	No 9	No 10	No 11	No 12	No 13	No 14	No 15
1	-1	-1	-1	-1	8	3	5	8	5	7	8	7	3	8	5	7	4	4	2
2	1	-1	-1	1	1	2	3	1	4	3	2	3	8	3	7	8	7	8	3
3	-1	1	-1	1	4	4	7	2	3	5	6	1	7	7	1	5	8	2	4
4	1	1	-1	-1	5	5	1	3	2	1	5	2	1	5	4	1	2	6	1
5	-1	-1	1	1	2	7	8	4	7	2	4	6	2	1	8	4	1	3	5
6	1	1	1	-1	6	6	2	5	8	4	3	5	5	2	6	2	6	1	6
7	-1	1	1	-1	7	1	6	6	6	8	7	8	6	4	2	3	5	5	7
8	1	1	1	1	3	8	4	7	1	6	1	4	4	6	3	6	3	7	8

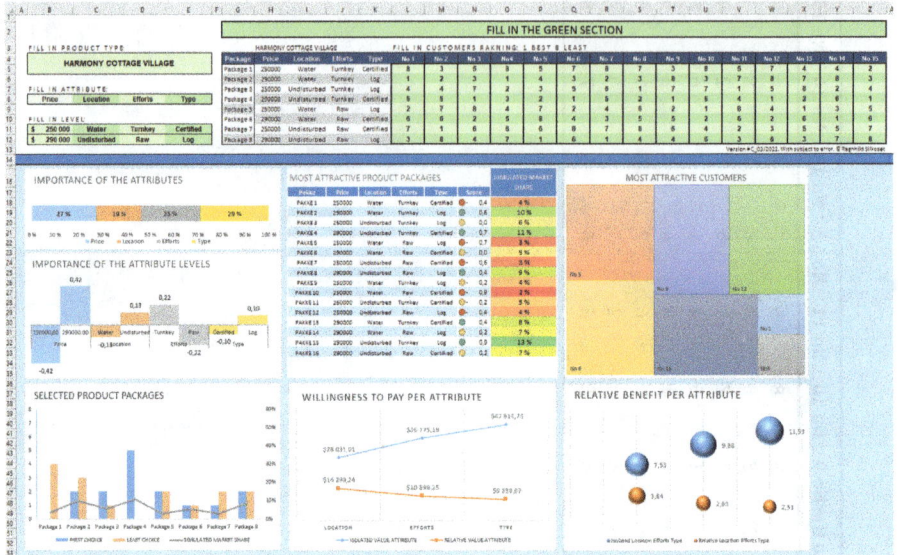

Figure 3.24: Dashboard.

Step 4: Calculate the Economic Effect

In the dashboard for the Excel analysis of "Harmony Cottage Village" I illustrate a few models to demonstrate the opportunities. The first, Figure 3.25, "Importance of the attributes," shows the estimated importance (from the regression analysis) of the attributes in a distribution of 100 percent. This makes it easy for the user of the dashboard to compare the values in perspective to each other.

The next, Figure 3.26, shows the importance of the levels of the attributes. This is the regression coefficient for each attribute, with the difference between the levels. Here, the values + and − are due to the way the data set is encoded.

To calculate which product packages are most attractive, we multiply the regression coefficients by the selected levels of product attributes. We design the colored circles and columns in Figure 3.27 by selecting *Conditional formatting* on the icon bar in Excel. Market share is calculated using the utility function described earlier in the chapter. The colors are created by choosing *Conditional formatting* on the icon bar in Excel.

Most attractive customers, Figure 3.28, are calculated by summing the regression coefficients for the product package attributes multiplied by the inverse of the customers' ranking, plus intercept (beta 0). The ranking of the numbers shows which customers have selected the most optimal product packages.

Next, the selected product packages graph summarizes the ranking and reports how many respondents have chosen the various product packages as their first choice and their last choice (see Figure 3.29).

Willingness to pay per attribute is calculated by estimating the utility value per price range multiplied by the utility value of the attributes. Individual estimates do not consider the other attributes, while relative estimates do (see Figure 3.30).

Relative utility per attribute illustrates the score the customers have on the various attributes (see Figure 3.31).

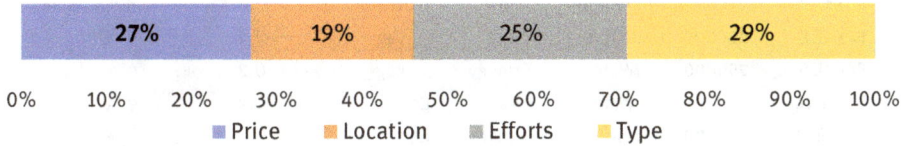

Figure 3.25: Importance of the Attributes.

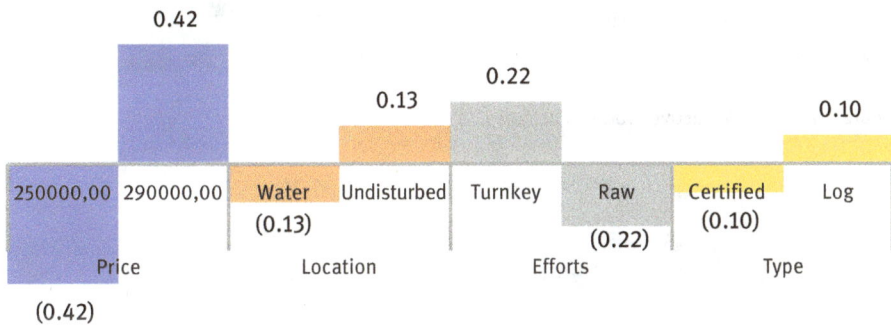

Figure 3.26: The Importance of the Levels.

Pakke	Price	Location	Efforts	Type	Score		SIMULATED MARKET SHARE
PAKKE 1	250000	Water	Turnkey	Certified	● -	0,4	4 %
PAKKE 2	290000	Water	Turnkey	Log	●	0,6	10 %
PAKKE 3	250000	Undisturbed	Turnkey	Log	○	0,0	6 %
PAKKE 4	290000	Undisturbed	Turnkey	Certified	●	0,7	11 %
PAKKE 5	250000	Water	Raw	Log	● -	0,7	3 %
PAKKE 6	290000	Water	Raw	Certified	○ -	0,0	5 %
PAKKE 7	250000	Undisturbed	Raw	Certified	● -	0,6	3 %
PAKKE 8	290000	Undisturbed	Raw	Log	●	0,4	9 %
PAKKE 9	250000	Water	Turnkey	Log	○ -	0,2	4 %
PAKKE 10	250000	Water	Raw	Certified	● -	0,9	2 %
PAKKE 11	250000	Undisturbed	Turnkey	Certified	○ -	0,2	5 %
PAKKE 12	250000	Undisturbed	Raw	Log	● -	0,4	4 %
PAKKE 13	290000	Water	Turnkey	Certified	●	0,4	8 %
PAKKE 14	290000	Water	Raw	Log	○	0,2	7 %
PAKKE 15	290000	Undisturbed	Turnkey	Log	●	0,9	13 %
PAKKE 16	290000	Undisturbed	Raw	Certified	○	0,2	7 %

Figure 3.27: Most Attractive Product Packages.

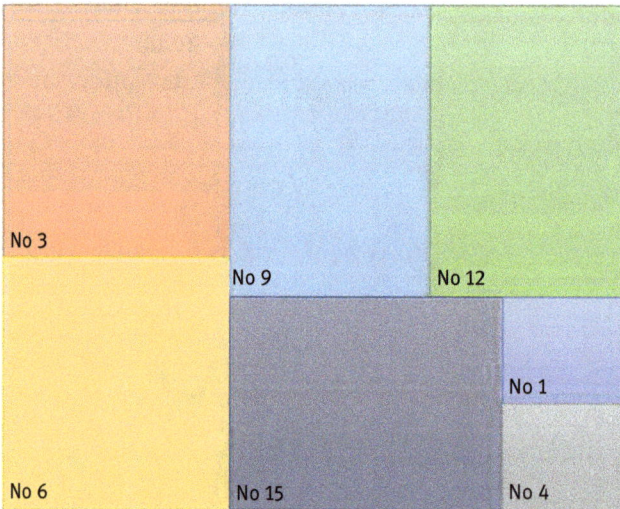

Figure 3.28: The Most Attractive Customers.

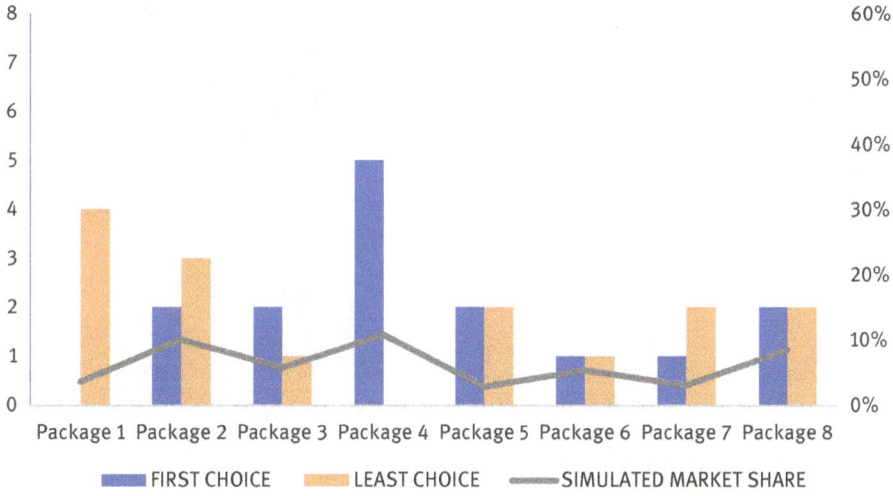

Figure 3.29: Selected Product Packages.

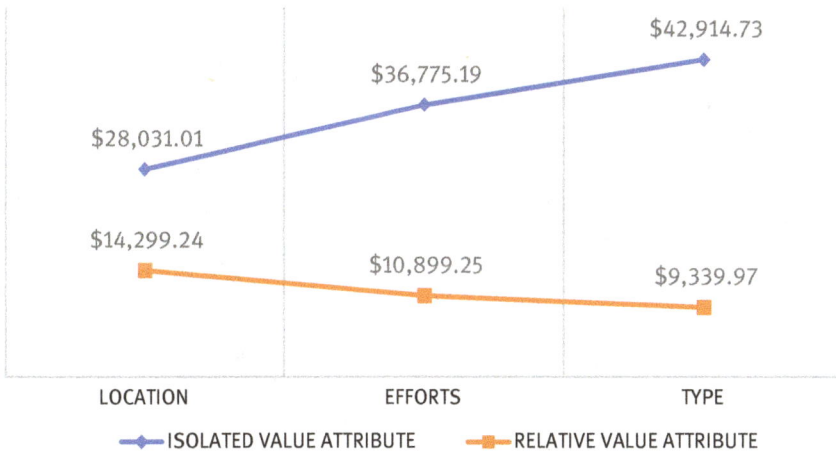

Figure 3.30: Willingness to Pay per Attribute.

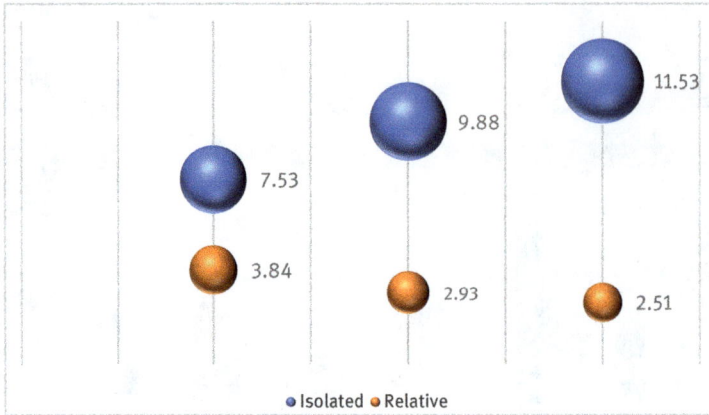

Figure 3.31: Relative Utility per Attribute.

Chapter 4
Different Prices for the Same Products

Introduction

In this chapter, I will show how one can vary the prices of products that are apparently equal or similar to each other. To do this, I have divided the chapter into four parts. First, I discuss how you can vary the price of a product based on the buyer of the product. If one has no or little experience with pricing strategy, this is a common method to use for price discrimination. The second and another common way to vary prices is through localization. The third way describes the opportunities to vary prices based on different ways of designing the product. Examples here include how the product is used, or how large quantities are purchased. Finally, I have included price variation based on the time when the product is purchased. This is everything from seasonal variations to frequency of use.

Price segmentation means that you charge *different prices* for products that are equal or similar. This seems intuitively impossible, but I will go through several factors that are crucial for such a strategy to work. Segmentation means dividing the customers into groups where the customers are equal within their group, but different between groups. Customer segmentation is usually based on the customer's age and gender. As I will show in this chapter, such demographic factors are often less effective than other types of segmentation. Examples of the latter include product design, time of purchase, and location.

Simple examples of demographics include the lower price of train tickets for children, students, and seniors. Cinema tickets vary between children and adults, and ski resorts offer lower prices on annual passes to those with a local address. More subtle examples are different menus at some restaurants in tourist areas, with higher prices for guests, and lower prices for locals. In addition, there might be big differences in flight ticket prices depending on how far in advance you book your ticket. In other words, we differ according to our willingness to pay.

To be able to maneuver different prices on similar products, one is dependent on what are called "price fences." A price fence is strong when it is based on fixed criteria that customers must meet to qualify for lower prices. Two examples of such factors are age (children, seniors) and geography (coupons from local newspapers). A weak price fence will not always be able to separate the customer segments from each other. An example of this is when electronics are cheaper in one state than in a neighboring state. A second example is education status (students get lower prices), where many transportation companies have set an age limit of 30 years to continue being considered a student. Weak price fences can lead to profitability leaks.

https://doi.org/10.1515/9783110987102-004

Varying prices between customer groups give room for extra earnings. But this also comes with high risk. Wrongdoing can lead to furious customers because they think they have been treated unfairly. I have described this risk and how it is handled in Chapter 7, which is entitled "Unfair price!" Figure 4.1, which illustrates prices of Coca-Cola cans, demonstrates how the price can vary depending on geography.

Online store	Super-market	Grocery store	Gasoline station located at a highway	Gasoline station located outside a highway	Bar	Hotel	Beach vending machine
$1.95	$1.50	$1.95	$2.40	$2.25	$2.50	$3.00	$3.00

Figure 4.1: Example of Variation in the Price of a Coca-Cola can be based on the Point of Sale.

It is important to understand the difference between price sensitivity, willingness to pay, and price elasticity.
- *Price sensitivity* is a characteristic of the buyer or customer. Some people are more sensitive to price changes, and this can vary between different products and services. It can also vary within a product through the combination of different attributes or from one purchase point to another. High price sensitivity refers to customers who are price-conscious, while with low price sensitivity, price is not the main driver for purchases.
- *Willingness to pay* is also a characteristic of the buyer or customer. A measure of willingness to pay shows how much value a consumer has put on a product or service. Willingness to pay is measured in the form of money.
- *Price elasticity* is the percentage change in demand divided by the percentage change in price. In other words, this is about the aggregate demand for a product and the shape of the demand curve. Price elasticity is usually negative, i.e., you buy less of a product if the price increases. There are exceptions: for example, for unique luxury products where high prices increase demand. When it comes to price elasticity, it is common to distinguish between product categories and brand categories. An example of a price change in product categories is when all petrol stations increase their petrol prices, we only buy slightly less petrol. If only one brand player, for example Shell, changes the price at all their petrol stations, it will have a big effect on their sales. The calculation of price elasticity and cross-price elasticity is described in the last chapter in this book.

In the following sections, I will review the main principles for price segmentation. I have chosen to categorize the principles into four parts, namely attributes of the buyer, location, product, and time (see Figure 4.2).

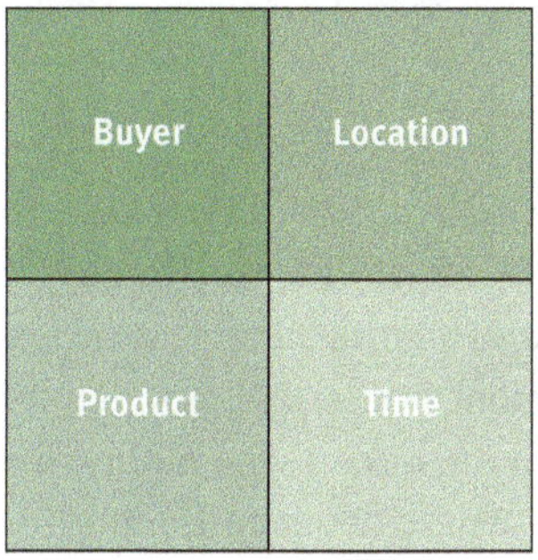

Figure 4.2: Four Categories within Price Segmentation.

The Buyer

Segmentation is well known in marketing and is especially important when it comes to price. Customers have different needs and different willingness to pay. By varying the price based on these segmentation criteria, one will utilize in a better way the potential for earnings in a market. The logic is that it is better to offer different prices in a market with different willingness to pay rather than offering the same price to everyone. *The solution is to create a system that makes sure the buyers must qualify for the lower prices.* This prevents everyone from choosing the cheapest solution. An example of such qualification is age.

Price segmentation based on attributes of the buyer is often the simplest as this is easy to identify and accept. For example, hairdressers have a lower price for haircuts for children because the parents would alternatively choose to cut the children's hair themselves. By reducing the price, they ensure that these customers will not disappear, while at the same time this cost reduction does not ruin the mainstream market. The most important thing about this type of price segmentation is that the criteria are *predefined*, *objective*, and *easily identifiable*. This is to prevent a negotiating practice that negatively impacts the mainstream market. This fits together with what was described in the previous section, i.e., that the criteria for price determination must be clear and understood throughout the company. If someone chooses to reduce the price for customers who complain of a high price, it could be devastating for the whole price strategy of the company.

Examples of customer attributes that can be mapped include the following:
1. Age
2. Gender
3. Education

4. Position
5. Income
6. Social status
7. Family situation
8. Life stage
9. Occupation

Note that the price segmentation requires that the attributes of the buyer *lead to different willingness to pay*. If the attributes do not affect the willingness to pay, it would be wrong to segment prices. Recent research shows that customers are very skeptical about their buying history being used to segment prices [20]. To identify which attributes of the buyer are decisive and relevant in the price segmentation for the company's specific products or services, one is completely dependent on documented information. This I discussed in Chapter 3, which measures customers' reactions to price changes.

The Location

If customers shop in different areas, they can be segmented based on location. This is a very common way of segmenting prices, and well-known examples include various outlets in the retail and service industries. An electrical store with shops in many places can vary the prices of its goods depending on the different geographical areas. The customers willingness to pay in the geographical area is often used as a reason. Remember, however, that customers talk to each other, so any price discrimination must be legal and perceived as fair. Localization often has weak price fences. Localization also differentiates between sales in the physical store and online sales.

A common practice is that online sales are priced below products in physical stores. The argument is often that store sales include professional expertise, personal advice, and guidance, which helps to increase customers' perceived value. It is up to each individual business if they want to have different prices in store and online. Detailed information on prices in e-commerce is presented in Chapter 10.

Areas where several competing companies are co-located put price pressure on the products. This is because the effort and cost customers spend finding and choosing an alternative product is lower. In several cases, this leads to chain stores having lower prices in urban areas than in more rural areas. But be careful. Sometimes one can read a newspaper story about angry customers who feel exploited by this kind of price variation within established branded chains. This is because customers who do not perceive the price variation as fair feel punished and thus give emotional responses.

Location can also be shown through much simpler examples. When you buy tickets to a performance, concert, or sports competition, the prices vary depending on where in the hall or arena you want to sit (see Figure 4.3). Seats with good sound and a good overview are often far more expensive than tickets further away from the center of events. These are clear criteria for price variation that customers are used to from before, and where one voluntarily buys oneself a good place rather than being punished for something you cannot control.

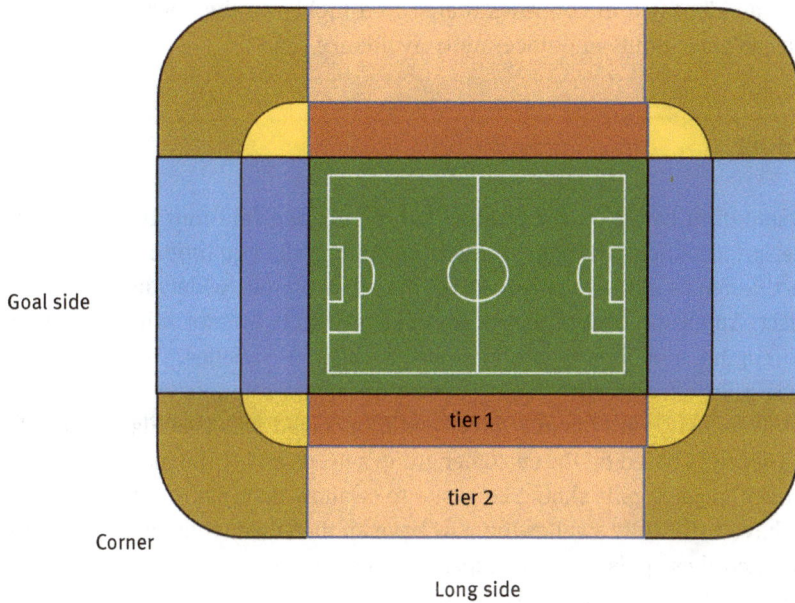

Seating:	Price group	Seating:	Price group	Seating:	Price group
Corner side tier 1:	3	Long side tier 1:	1	Goal side tier 1:	2
Corner side tier 2:	4	Long side tier 2:	2	Goal side tier 2:	3

Figure 4.3: Ticket Prices Based on Location.

Examples of attributes of localization that may affect the willingness to pay include:
1. location
2. city – rural area
3. population density
4. language
5. climate
6. distances
7. number of providers
8. borders

International trade often has price variation on their products. E-commerce, which is discussed in Chapter 10 of this book, is an example of this. Trade barriers in the form of customs duties, subsidies, quotas, and taxes affect the price of a product. In addition, there are shipping, insurance, and payment agreements. The challenge with international price segmentation is to segment entire countries. One and the same country, such as Italy, may have large inward differences in terms of willingness to pay. A study that mapped the popularity of apps in the App Store in 60 different countries showed a large degree of variation in price sensitivity. Higher price sensitivity was identified in countries that scored highly on the degree of cultural factors such as masculinity and uncertainty avoidance [21].

The Product

Price segmentation based on the product can be divided into four types, namely product design, product bundling, product use, and product quantity.

Product design as a price segmentation criterion is simple, widely used, and has a great effect. An example most people are familiar with is Tylenol, which is sold in different strengths, in different quantities, and in different varieties. There are round pills, oblong pills, effervescent tablets, suppositories, oral solutions, and dispersible tablets, intravenously, with banana flavor and film-coated pills (see Figure 4.4). All variants have prices based on the customer group's needs and willingness to pay. For example, the elongated pills should be easier to swallow than the round pills. Thus, those who have a difficulty swallowing pills have an increased willingness to pay for this benefit, and these pills are more expensive. It should be noted that the different product variants do not necessarily have different production costs.

For price variation based on product design, one piece of advice is to offer a low-cost version that is *insufficient* to meet the needs of customers with a higher willingness to pay, but which has one acceptable price for customers with a lower willingness to pay. In this way, one pays for a good instead of being punished for one's own inadequacy.

Examples of product design attributes that may affect willingness to pay include:
1. superior performance
2. better operational reliability
3. additional attributes
4. lower operating costs
5. super or unique attributes
6. higher startup costs
7. faster and better service

Price segmentation through product design is especially easy when selling services. Airlines have used the product design strategy for many years. The market consists

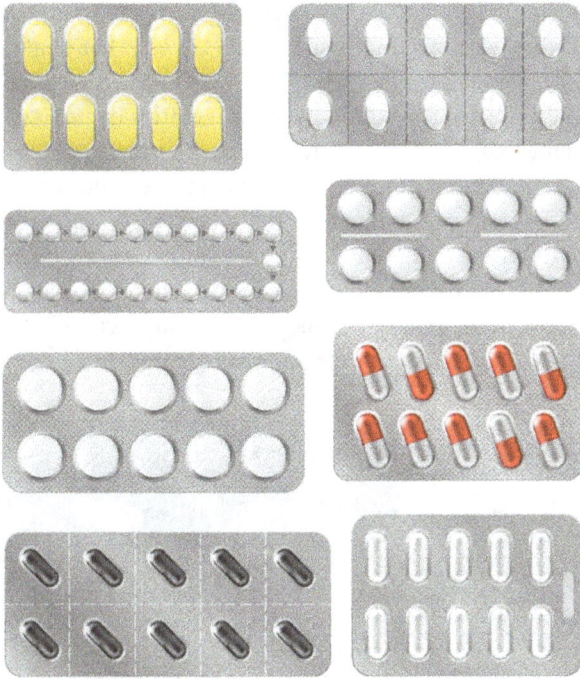

Figure 4.4: Variants of Painkiller Pills with Different Prices.

of business travelers with a high willingness to pay, and leisure travelers with a lower willingness to pay. Economy tickets are cheaper but have fewer benefits associated with them. They cannot be changed, have less luggage included, you get less help if something unforeseen should happen on the trip, you do not have access to fast-track check-in or a lounge, you have less comfortable seats, your luggage comes last on the luggage belt (at least in theory), and so on. For business travelers, time is often a key factor and triggers a higher willingness to pay. Business travelers want to have the extra services available, even though they do not necessarily know if or when they will need them. Therefore, price variation on airline tickets works in the market. With increased price competition between airlines, however, the boundaries between which customers get access to the various benefits are floating. We experience categories such as economy-plus, business-smart, business-pro, and a whole range of variants within these.

The result is that those customers who originally had the highest willingness to pay no longer feel that they get the extra services they pay for but must stand in an equal line with everyone else. Thus, the basis for the price variation on product design disappears, and there is a risk that everyone chooses the low-price variant.

Product bundling is a well-known way of segmenting the price. Newspapers package digital and paper editions at a total price that is lower than if the products were purchased separately. Therefore, many people choose the package solution over the single purchase, and thus earnings increase (see Figure 4.5). Car dealerships offer car sales with various campaigns, be they trade-in campaigns, metallic-paint campaigns, winter-ready cars, funding campaigns, accessories campaigns, technological performance campaigns, or premium promotions. The variation is almost infinite. The purpose of product bundling is to offer a good trade to customers with a lower willingness to pay, while at the same time those customers who want freedom of choice get the opportunity to achieve it. Customers with a lower willingness to pay often choose to spend more money on buying the product package rather than buying a single product. The reason is what we call "transaction benefits." I will return to this in more detail in Chapter 9 on psychological pricing.

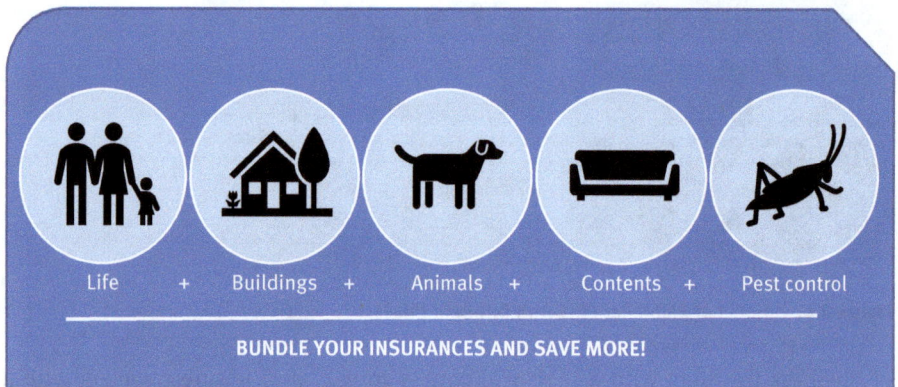

| Life | + | Buildings | + | Animals | + | Contents | + | Pest control |

BUNDLE YOUR INSURANCES AND SAVE MORE!

Figure 4.5: Product Bundling.

There are several ways to bundle products. Products that are bundled can be *complementary*. This means that they have a natural connection, such as a car and a towbar. The bundling can also be *cross-selling*. This means that they are used simultaneously, such as, for example, shampoo and conditioner. Web sales have easy access to product bundling by utilizing input visibility based on the algorithm estimation from products that have been purchased at the same time by previous customers. Thirdly, bundling can consist of *optional extras*, for example installation, service, and insurance. One example is that purchases over $50 receive free shipping. Product bundling can be hidden from the customers, even though this is often not equally effective in varying the price. If a hotel, for example, charges $250 per night and $10 for one bottle of exclusive water, most customers would probably see it as robbery. If the hotel, however, charges $260 per night and the exclusive water is included, it is perceived as a very good purchase.

Research shows that the products you choose to promote in the product bundling are of great importance for how attractive the product package is. In one experiment, a paper folder and a box of chocolates were packed. When product bundling was

presented as a hedonistic value, meaning that you got the chocolate with the purchase, 82 percent responded that they were willing to buy (see Figure 4.6). When
product bundling was presented as a utility value, where you got an additional
cheap paper folder in the deal, 52 percent of the participants responded that they
were interested in buying. And when product bundling was presented as money
saved, 61 percent said yes to buying it. This variation may be an indication that customers often feel guilt when they buy products only for their own pleasure, and the
way it is packaged, thereby affecting how prominent this guilt feeling is [22]. Note,
however, that customers do not feel the same guilt when buying a gift for others,
such as flowers, wine, or subscriptions. One possible product bundling is therefore to
offer a gift subscription together with a 50 percent discount on magazines for your
own use. For hybrid bundles, in which products and services are packaged together,
trials show that one can achieve higher willingness to pay for these compared to a
situation where the products and the services are sold separately [23]. The premise is
that the service part of the packages should be at a low level for cheaper package
options, and at a high level for premium packages. This is described in more detail in
Chapter 9 on psychological pricing.

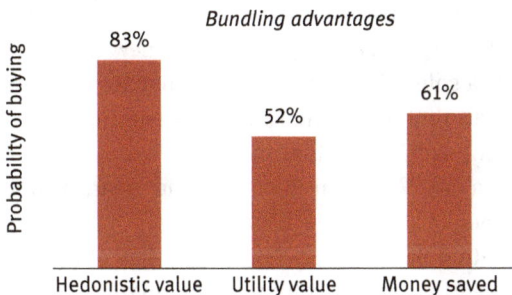

Figure 4.6: Probability of Purchase with Various Advantages of Product Bundling [22].

A further distinction is made between optional bundling and value-added bundling [4].
With *optional bundling*, you combine two or more products together at a fixed price.
The sum of this package is lower than the products purchased separately. Concert or-
ganizers offer packages with hotel accommodation and restaurant visits included in
the price. Restaurants offer pre-packaged three-, five-, and seven-course menus at a
lower price than if the dishes are purchased individually. Football teams sell season
tickets at a lower price than if the tickets are purchased for each match. Sports shops
sell skis, poles, bindings, and boots in ready-made packages. Meanwhile, the customers are free to buy these products individually. *Added-value bundling* adds to one or
another form of *extra value to customers with lower willingness to pay*. It is only this
group of customers who emphasize these additional benefits of having a value. This
prevents the contagion effect between groups with high and low willingness to pay.

An example of this is the packaging of a game along with a game console. Such digital products, where the extra production costs of the games are almost zero, are particularly applicable for product bundling [24]. Those with a higher willingness to pay choose to buy games they see as interesting, regardless of the product bundling. Those with a lower willingness to pay, on the other hand, buy the package and get the predetermined games with the purchase.

Product usage segments the price based on the value customers experience when using the product. Here, a distinction is made between two types: connection sales and metering [4]. *Tie-in sales* are about selling the main product cheaply, often below market price, while the use of the product is highly priced. Everyone knows about the sale of mobile phones, where the phones are often sold under the market price if you are willing to tie in to specific subscription arrangements with bindings. This is especially attractive to customers with low product knowledge. They choose such solutions to reduce their own risk. Other examples include the development we are now seeing in the car sales industry, where dealers offer subscription schemes with specific criteria for the number of kilometers for which the cars can be used (see *Care By Volvo*). Customers do not pay for the car, only the usage. This is therefore an offer far below the market price. The technological risk (see Chapter 2) and uncertainty within the reusability of new cars affect some customers when choosing a subscription solution despite the fact that the monthly payment is larger than the purchase of a new car.

When it comes to *metering*, this is a solution where customers pay for different usage of the product. The customer can rent a parking space in a parking garage monthly, or they can choose to pay for each individual parking. *Getaround* is an example of payment for the usage of a car. Variation in cars' brand, year, model, and location affects the customer segment's willingness to pay.

Product quantity is price segmentation based on how much you buy of a product. Here, a distinction is made between four types: volume, order quantity, incremental volume, and two-part pricing [4]. For *the volume* the price varies because customers who buy large quantities are often more cost-conscious than buyers of lower quantities. In addition, it is often attractive to retain large-volume customers because they are relatively cheaper to handle.

Volume discounts are common in the business market where large quantities are common. The volume discount is often calculated based on the transactions over a specific period, such as last year (see Figure 4.7). *The number of orders* refers to when the company has high fixed costs per order, such as warehousing costs, bundling, invoices, shipping, and personnel. The company has an incentive to stimulate customers to buy larger quantities per order rather than many small purchases. This is done by giving discounts to those customers who are willing to buy larger quantities than they *otherwise* would have done. *Incremental volume* is used in the business market. The buyers get a discount based on their volume range. This stimulates customers not to switch supplier underway. *Two-party pricing* refers to cases where the price is divided into two – a fixed price and a usage price. The cruise ship industry uses this price quite consciously. The cruise itself has one price where everything on board is included, i.e., accommodation, food, entertainment, and non-alcoholic drinks. On land you can choose to go free on your own without a guide, or you can take part in organized tours within different price ranges. These price adjustments ensure that more can afford to choose a cruise as a holiday type. This example, of course, applies to the old days, before the year 2020, when the cruise industry was still flourishing and there was no pandemic.

Concert Series Subscriptions

Gold series
Silver series
Bronze series
Classics
Create your own
Jubilee's concerts
Conductors recommendation

The **gold series** consists of 10 concerts.

Price levels for the gold series:
Price level 1: $345
Price level 2: $310
Price level 3: $240
Price level 4: $140

Figure 4.7: Subscriptions at the Concert Halls.

The Time

Items with a short shelf life or lack of stock, such as fresh products, fashion, experiences, and service, are critically important to manage in terms of time of purchase and consumption. Last year's fashion is sold at greatly reduced prices and sometimes at a loss, while old milk cannot even be given away for free. A rock concert cannot store unsold tickets.

Price segmentation based on time assumes that customers value the product differently based on time the of the day, week, season, or year. In stock trading, prices are delayed by 15 minutes, and you can buy so-called "snapshots" to get real-time data on stock prices if this is important for you. A restaurant has cheaper lunch dishes than dinner dishes. The reason is that the willingness to pay is higher in the evening. A theater offers cheaper matinee performances in the morning. These tickets are attractive to students and pensioners, who may have free time at this time of day, but who also have a lower willingness to pay. This does not destroy the main market in the evening, and you can make better use of the resources – which cannot be stored for later use. Moreover, research shows that when customers are under time pressure, they select individual products at lower prices rather than product bundles [25].

There are two main types of price segmentation based on time, namely peak load pricing and yield management pricing [4].

The objective of *peak load pricing* is to move the peak load demand into times of availability (see Figure 4.8). In other words, this has to do with capacity costs. Cities implement different prices to pass through the toll booth as a capacity cost. As most people drive through the toll booth at the working day's start and end, roads experience capacity problems. By increasing the price in the hectic period, customers can select the time range where the prices are lower. Another development is the new, electric smart power meters in all homes and businesses. This enables a differentiation of electricity consumption based on the load on the power grid. Those who have a lower willingness to pay for electricity are willing to start the washing machine at

Parking prices for different time zones

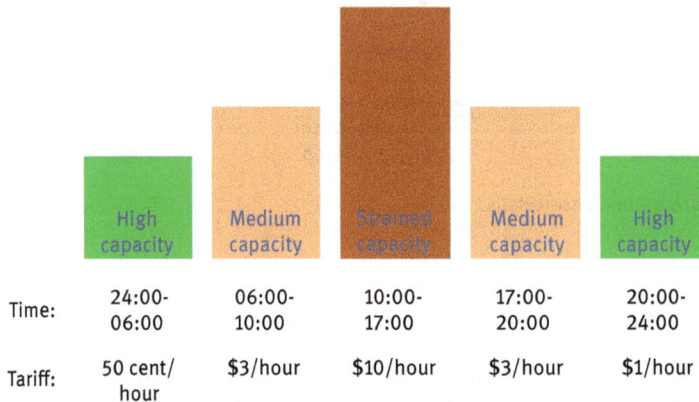

	High capacity	Medium capacity	Strained capacity	Medium capacity	High capacity
Time:	24:00-06:00	06:00-10:00	10:00-17:00	17:00-20:00	20:00-24:00
Tariff:	50 cent/hour	$3/hour	$10/hour	$3/hour	$1/hour

Figure 4.8: Peak Load Pricing.

a more unfavorable time than those who are not concerned about the price of electricity. This improved capacity utilization saves network companies large investments in new lines and power cables. However, if the price is set too low in line with low-capacity costs, one can quickly experience the opposite peak load.

Yield management pricing is used when the capacity is exhausted and companies risk missing sales. Everyone wants to go on holiday during the school holidays, and kennel places for dogs are quickly sold out. At the same time, the kennels have spare capacity in the low season. By offering lower prices during the low season, they might turn the demand so that those who can travel at less popular times receive incentives to choose this. This time perspective can also apply where you operate with shorter time periods. With an airline that has the greatest demand for aircraft seats from business travelers on Mondays and Fridays, you can use the price mechanism to reward those who can choose another time on weekdays. Thus, they do not miss the sale but get the relief spread over the time. And the tour operator will find that the seats are sold out before the hotel rooms. They can even out this capacity by offering a much cheaper week two of the holiday. Total earnings increase, while the load is evened out.

Summary

This chapter has been about how to vary the price between products that are apparently similar or like each other. The chapter was divided into four parts. The first concerned the variation in the price of a product based on conditions that had to do with the actual buyer of the product. This method is easy to use, but often not as effective as the others described in the chapter. The second method, which is also a common way of varying prices, is through localization. Different geographical locations affect markets with different willingness to pay. The third way to have price variation concerns different ways of adapting the product. Different design variants of a product often provide good opportunities for price variations. Finally, I included price variation based on the time the product was purchased. This applies to everything from seasonal variations to frequency of use.

Chapter 5
Different Prices for the Same Customers

Introduction

While the previous chapter discussed how one can vary the price between otherwise similar *products*, this chapter will explain how one can vary the prices for the same *customer*. To do so I have divided the chapter into two main parts. The first part deals with the financial impacts on customers' willingness to pay. The second part deals with the perceptual influences on the willingness to pay. Each element includes a rating, which is drawn from the work by Nagle and Müller [4].

It is easy to imagine that customers' willingness to pay is fixed and cannot be changed. The price sensitivity indicates that an increase in price reduces the number who will buy the product. It sounds perhaps illogical that one can get one customer to *volunteer* to pay more than strictly necessary, but I will give several examples showing that this is fully possible and even keeps them happy.

To start the thought process, look at the phone that is probably next to you. How many times have you switched between different mobile phone manufacturers lately? For example, from iPhone to Samsung? Probably not many times. Having tried once, you quickly finds that it takes a long time and creates much irritation to learn how the new phone works. You want to avoid this, and this implies that you have a higher pain threshold (read lower price sensitivity) before you decide to swap to a cheaper brand. Maybe you don't even bother to try. This pain threshold means that mobile phone manufacturers can increase the price further before customers take the step to switch brand. This effect is called the "switching cost effect" and is one of the examples we will go through in this chapter [4].

Financial Impacts on Customers' Willingness to Pay

Financial impacts on customers' willingness to pay are about the resources required in the price assessments. In this section, we will take a closer look at four types of financial impacts on customers' willingness to pay, namely the switching cost effect, difficult comparison effect, expenditure effect, and end-benefit effect. Under each point is the pointed question one must ask to identify the effect on the customers [4].

Switching Cost Effect

The higher the costs a customer experiences when switching to a different product, the higher the willingness to pay the customers have for the product [4]. A distinction

https://doi.org/10.1515/9783110987102-005

is made between three types of switching costs, namely the direct switching costs, the financial switching costs, and the relational switching costs. The *direct switching costs* are about costs that apply by switching between manufacturers or brands. Examples are time and money. If a company changes its entire storage system, they must identify alternatives as well as calculating downtime and organizational consequences and strain, and not least, the time it takes to learn up the new system. These costs might result in the decision to postpone the entire decision.

The *financial exchange costs* include, for example, fees, the cost of breach of contract, establishment fee, and lock-in period. This is something banks use quite deliberately in their marketing, in that they offer to pay the fees and costs for you if you transfer your loan to their bank.

The *relational exchange costs* are the psychological effects of breaking a relationship and entering a new one. Local banks know that many of their customers are willing to continue with them as their bank for the reason that they have been part of their life throughout their childhood. Such affective bonds can be very strong, and it can feel painful to break them [26]. Switching cost results in a lower willingness to switch supplier. This in turn means that price sensitivity decreases more the higher the switching costs. In other words, with high switching costs, we accept higher price changes than we would otherwise have done before we chose to switch products.

Ratings:
- To what extent have customers made investments (both financial and psychological) that they must repeat if they change products?
- How long are customers bound by these investments?

Difficult Comparison Effect

The more difficult it is to compare the different products, the higher the willingness to pay [4]. A distinction is made between three levels of difficult comparison, namely a comparison of brands, new entrants in the market, and pack size.

A *brand* symbolizes an added value, an image, that customers value. This added value is difficult to compare and allows brands to charge a higher price for identical products. Brands affect the ability to compare product attributes. In grocery stores, you often see the chains' private labels, such as Great Value spaghetti from Walmart, on the same shelf as the manufacturers' brands, such as Barilla. Studies show that this increases sales of private labels [27], and the reason is that the location makes it easier to compare products. The opposite also applies. Customers are less sensitive to the price (e.g., higher willingness to pay) of well-known brands when it is more difficult to compare alternatives. In addition, the brand effect has an impact on comparability.

New entrants in the market encounter resistance from existing players who want to protect their market share. This is used quite consciously by providers of mobile subscriptions. Comparing different subscriptions is almost impossible, and thus customers tolerate higher price increases before they take the step of changing subscription. When the information-gathering process is demanding, price sensitivity is reduced. Uncertainty leads to resistance to change. As an example, the Chase Bank has a complicated price list with a variety of different amounts for its services (see https://www.chase.com/content/dam/chasecom/en/checking/documents/clear_simple_guide_total.pdf).

The size of the products also makes price comparisons more difficult. Unit sizes such as kilograms and meters are easy, and standardized price units are required to be stated on the price label. But how much is a unit of dental time? Prices for services are more difficult to compare because they are not easy to quantify. Service providers are required to provide a general price list to anyone who asks. But customers cannot easily know in advance what specific services they are going to need. This means that the prices for the main services are compared, such as the actual hourly price at the dentist, while the prices for other products, such as anesthesia and X-rays, are more difficult to compare. Therefore, one has a lower price sensitivity for these extra activities.

Ratings:

- How difficult is it for customers to compare the different products?
- Can the attributes of the product be observed, or must it be used before anyone knows anything about them?
- What percentage of the market has positive experiences with your product compared to the competition?
- Is the product complicated? Does it require additional knowledge for customers to be able to compare the attributes?
- Are the prices between the different products easy to compare, or do they have some combinations that make the comparison difficult?

Expenditure Effect

The larger the share of the income a purchase makes, the more sensitive customers are to the price [4]. The expenditure effect increases the willingness to invest in the time to compare information and prices, and to actively seek means to reduce their costs.

In these cases, it is important to remember that a customer may have a completely different basis for comparison than they have with smaller purchases. Maybe the choice is between a vacation trip to Florida or buying a new car. At the same time, the transaction is of greater importance, so the buyers are not necessarily willing to compromise on the desired attributes.

From a price point of view, this means that the higher the proportion of a budget a purchase accounts for, the more price sensitive is the customer. When the purchase constitutes a small share of the budget, the price is less important, and the willingness to pay increases.

In practice, this also means that the same product can have a completely different price sensitivity based on the volume the customers buy. If you buy a pack of eggs for one cake, this is one completely insignificant cost, and you are not concerned by the price whatsoever. If, on the other hand, you buy 2 tons of eggs a year, the price is very important.

Ratings:

- What is the nominal product cost ($), and what proportion does this make up of the household's income (percent)?

Shared Cost Effect

It is always easier to spend other people's money than your own! Price sensitivity is reduced when customers use other people's money to pay for a product [4]. In Figure 5.1, I show four different ways in which price and benefit vary depending on the source and the purpose of the financing. Such a table is of course general and does not apply in every case, but it can still give an indication of how price sensitivity is affected.

Source of the finance

		Own money	Others money
Purpose of the finance	For yourself	**1.** Moderate price sensitivity High benefit sensitivity	**2.** Low price sensitivity High benefit sensitivity
	To others	**3.** Moderate price sensitivity Low benefit sensitivity	**4.** Low price sensitivity Low benefit sensitivity

Figure 5.1: Different Sensitivity to the Source and Purpose of Money [4].

In *cell 1*, one uses one's own money on oneself. This leads to more concern about the value you get for your money, while being aware of how much money you spend. Benefiting from every penny is important. For airplane tickets, one is more willing to travel at inconvenient times when tickets are cheaper. At the same time, one is not willing to travel to a less attractive destination even if flights there are cheaper.

In *cell 2*, the conditions are lighter. Here you spend other people's money on yourself. The willingness to pay increases at the same time as you want the maximum value based on the transaction. If you are going to fly in connection with your job, you are inclined to choose the departure time that fits you best, while the price becomes less important. The price of the tickets will be refunded by the employer. This, in turn, forces companies to set $ limits to prevent overconsumption. Examples include requirements for ticket type and the maximum amount you can spend.

In *cell 3*, you spend your own money on others. Examples include gifts to others. You spend a lot of time finding a gift that benefits the recipient, while at the same time being concerned about the price of the item itself. Perceived benefit per dollar is important in these transactions. At the same time, the benefit changes to be the recipient's perception.

In *cell 4*, you spend other people's money on others. As we can see, one is less concerned by either price or value for money. Rather, one is more concerned with getting the trade done. Extensive use of discounts will have little effect on this type of transaction.

Ratings:

- Does the customer pay for everything or just for parts?
- How big a share of the payment does the customer pay by themselves versus others?

Perceptual Influences on Customers' Willingness to Pay

Perceptual influences on customers' willingness to pay are about the subjective perception of price variations. Here we shall enter four effects, namely price-quality effect, unique value effect, substitute effect, and final distribution effect.

Price-Quality Effect

Imagine that you are about to buy clothes. In the store you find two options: one sweater for $100 or three sweaters for a total of $100. Most people immediately think that the three sweaters are of lower quality and may not be worth the money. Let us further imagine that you buy all four sweaters. A few years later you must clean out your closet. Which sweaters are the easiest to throw away, and which are left in the closet year after year?

Customers thus do not use price just as a measure of how much they must sacrifice to get a product or service. The prices are also like a signal effect on the quality of the products. The connection has been tested in several studies, and it has been found that price is an important quality indicator when there is quality variation within the product class, when it is assumed that low quality entails a risk, or when other information (such as brand names) is missing, which affects the ability to assess the quality before buying [6]. Price in this context is an extrinsic signal (i.e., outside the product itself), along with the brand, the package, its reputation, and origins. An intrinsic signal (i.e., the product itself) is the inherent attributes of the product. Well-informed customers put more emphasis on the intrinsic (the actual) attributes of a product. Customers with particularly high product knowledge also use price as a signal of quality because these customers are familiar with the quality variations. Examples include wine connoisseurs and the price of wine. This means that buyers are less sensitive to the price of a product when the price signals quality.

Remember that the opposite is also true. Successful chains that have a low-price strategy, such as Walmart, Aldo, and Dollar General, lead to increased price sensitivity and customers accept lower quality given that they get a good price.

Quality can be divided into different types, including image and symbolism, exclusive prestige, and average quality. In such contexts, the choice of quality reflects personality. One example is the platinum credit card, which symbolizes prestige and exclusivity in that others cannot afford the fees or have an income that is lower than the qualification for the card. Another form of exclusivity is first-class travel on aircraft. It's probably not inconceivable that anyone buying such tickets does so to avoid sitting next to a toddler who is crying.

In luxury markets, the common practice is to not show prices visibly. Recent research, however, does not support this and shows that visible prices have a positive effect on the perception of luxury, brand uniqueness, and the product's eye-catching uniqueness [28]. This affects the desire to buy the product. A second question is how the perception of luxury starts and stops on the price scale. One study found a continuum from the "happy few" to the many less privileged. This extreme heterogeneity across consumers is good news for luxury groups. Such heterogeneity provides a great choice for development strategies from traditional luxury to new luxury [29].

Ratings:
- Is prestige an important component of the product?
- Does the product increase in value if it is unavailable to a certain customer group?
- Is the product of unknown quality, and are there any reliable ways to detect the quality?

Unique Value Effect

Buyers are less price sensitive to products that seem to have unique attributes that set them apart from competing products [27]. The perception of the value of the attributes varies with the life cycle of the products. For products with short life cycles, such as fashion, value depends on a continuous development of the products to fit with the fashion scene. The price sensitivity for new products is thus low. For products with a longer life cycle, such as PC manufacturers, the value effect is to fit the product to different customer segments that value the attributes differently. The goal of the unique value effect is to influence customers to be willing to pay a higher price for these attributes, rather than choosing a cheaper option in the market.

Typical examples of unique value include Heinz ketchup and Coca-Cola. Both base their products on secret recipes that create uniqueness and thus increase the willingness to pay for the products.

Ratings:
– Which products do our customers compare our products with?
– How do our customers perceive our products as different from those of our competitors?
– Which attributes are the customers most concerned by when they choose this kind of product?

Substitute Effect

The substitute effect is about the price of alternative products. Customers are more price sensitive to products that they perceive as being higher priced than competing products [4]. The keyword here is "perceive." Some customers will perceive the price as significantly higher, while other customers see the difference as marginal. The variation can be caused by the purchasing situation or available time, as well as customers' needs. An effective way to handle the substitute effect is to introduce an expensive product for comparison. An example is Tesla, which compares itself to sports cars, not other electric cars.

New customers or customers with low market knowledge are less able to compare products. This makes these customers willing to pay a higher price. Examples include cafes in famous destinations. Customers know they are paying a premium but choose to do so rather than spend time finding alternatives.

Ratings:
– What options are customers usually aware of when considering a purchase?
– To what extent are customers familiar with the price of the alternatives?
– How are customers affected by the price of alternative products?

End-Benefit Effect

Imagine that you are about to brush up on your bathroom and get a price estimate of $25,000. Let us say that based on your financial capability, competitive comparison, and knowledge, you choose to accept the offer. You look forward to getting the job done and focus all your attention on the finished product, a new, beautiful bathroom.

This is an example of the end-benefit effect. In such a situation one ignores the individual prices, such as the price of shower handles, and accepts to a greater extent higher prices when profiled as a finished product. If, on the other hand, you had only changed the shower handle, you would have spent more time looking at alternatives and different prices of these specifically.

Other examples of the end-benefit effect are when arranging special events, such as a wedding, baptism, funeral, or a romantic dinner for two. In such cases, it feels uncomfortable exploiting discounts, coupons, or negotiating a price reduction. The emotional nature of these transactions makes one perceive the prices as acceptable without asking questions.

Ratings:
- Which end benefit do the customers want to achieve through the product?
- How price sensitive are customers to the cost of the end product?
- What share of the end benefits constitutes the price of the products?
- In what way can the products be repositioned with the customer as an end benefit?

Summary

The purpose of this chapter has been to describe how to charge different prices to the same customer. To explain this, I have distinguished between financial and perceptual influences on customers' willingness to pay. The financial impacts on customers' willingness to pay are the switching cost effect, the difficult comparability effect, the consumption effect, and the shared cost effect. The perceptual influences were the price-quality effect, unique value effect, substitute effect, and end-benefit effect.

Chapter 6
From Price Competition to Price War!

Introduction

A price war is the result of a price competition that has taken an aggressive turn. A price war arises when a price pressure forces the other competitors to follow [30]. In the competition, the focus is only on prices, and over time this can lead to bankruptcies and closures. In this chapter, I will show how companies can handle such aggressive price competitions. The chapter deals with step-by-step solutions for dealing with price wars. Then it describes different phases and reactions to a price war. The chapter also describes what the result of a price war may be. Price wars are common in the grocery industry, and a separate section takes a closer look at research that has been done in this sector.

Price wars are characterized by a heavy focus on competition. Prices are pushed to an undesirable level, the competition violates the industry standards, and price reductions happen much faster than in conventional markets. In the long run, such low prices are not sustainable. This is especially so in oligopoly markets, i.e., markets with few providers, such as oil and food chains, where one experiences aggressive price wars. The reason is that in such markets, companies are often forced to match a competitor's price reductions [30].

Aggressive price wars often start with one of the actors thinking the prices in the market are too high, or that they are willing to "buy market shares" at the expense of margins. In addition, price wars occur more easily when competitors do not have confidence in each other, or do not know each other well [31].

It is an important goal to stop a price war before it starts [31]. Several companies continuously do this by regularly communicating the purpose, scope, and length of their price changes through mass media. In this way, competitors are made aware of the price changes and can develop their reaction patterns accordingly. One appeals, in other words, to cooperation with competitors. The most current example of this is how grocery stores plan their pricing promotions. Often when they offer a price promotion, they run heavy marketing campaigns explaining which products will be reduced, and how long this will last. In an oligopoly market, in which the grocery chains operate, it is often difficult for the other chains to be uninterested or indifferent to the price games. The reason they communicate through the mass media is because a direct price collaboration between companies is illegal. The legislation on this is described in the chapter on "Unfair price."

https://doi.org/10.1515/9783110987102-006

Steps in Dealing with Price Wars

Businesses should strive to keep price competition at a low level instead of joining or starting a price war. Figure 6.1 describes the steps for dealing with a price war. The recommendations below are based on a study from the Harvard Business Review [31], which has several recommendations for companies that are exposed to attempts at price wars, together with other relevant literature in the field [4].

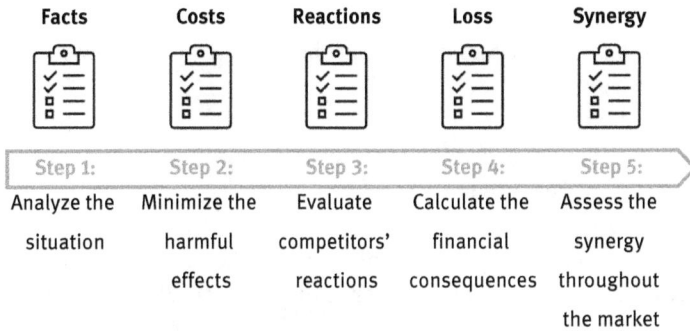

Facts	Costs	Reactions	Loss	Synergy

Step 1:	Step 2:	Step 3:	Step 4:	Step 5:
Analyze the situation	Minimize the harmful effects	Evaluate competitors' reactions	Calculate the financial consequences	Assess the synergy throughout the market

Figure 6.1: Steps in Dealing with Price Wars.

Step 1: Analyze the Situation

Are there responses that cost less than the estimated sales loss? It's easy to lose your head and forget that it is often better to lose sales in some product categories than engage in a fierce competition on price. If the price war threatens only a small part of your total market, it may be better to lose some revenue there rather than to extend the loss to apply to more products. One must also consider how long it is assumed that the loss is going to take place. If it is only for a short period of time, it may be wiser not to react. The analysis must investigate customers' price sensitivity and customer segments. Which customers are affected? Are these customers important? The analysis must also include business conditions such as cost structures, capabilities, and strategic position. The assessment must also look at what you can afford, what is important to maintain, and what is important to protect.

Step 2: Minimize the Harmful Effects

A company can actively reduce costs to minimize the damaging effects of a price war. This implies focusing on customer segments in the market. This is done by targeting the price cuts only to those customers who you think will react to the competitors' price cuts and leaving the rest untouched. You then focus on growing the volume that is at risk and let everything else be normal. Investigate whether you can direct the price cuts to some geographical areas or some product lines where the competitor has more to lose than you. Remember that the goal is not always to defend the sales that are lost, but to avoid losing sales in other important parts or areas. An unfriendly strategy is to let the other customers of the competitors know that they are being treated unfairly, that other customers get much lower prices than them.

Then, focus on your competitive advantages to increase the value of the products as an alternative to match the price cut. Often this is a far better strategy. Compete on quality and value and tell customers about the risks of buying low-priced products.

Step 3: Evaluate Competitors' Reactions

If you choose to match the price cut, it is important to predict the next move from the competitors. Will they respond to re-establish the price differences? Will the price spiral just go further and further down? Perhaps price cuts are the competitor's only way to acquire customers. This can make them willing to stretch themselves very far. Perhaps is it smarter to guarantee an equal price rather than setting the price lower. It can also be complicated to interpret and understand prices, something I have shown several examples of in this book. As an example, product bundling or second-price combinations make it more difficult to compete on price alone.

Step 4: Calculate the Financial Consequences

An important element that is often forgotten in a period of hectic price wars is calculating the economic consequences of a price war. An analysis will show whether the sum of all the measures you put into operation justifies what you would lose in a potential sale. Such an analysis must include the total costs – from a long-term perspective.

Step 5: Assess the Synergy Throughout the Market

Given that competitors manage to capture market share, what effect does this have on the company's position in other markets (geographic or product)? Are these threatened? Will the value of these markets justify the costs of responding? In some cases, the focus on the total market will change the competitive picture and action options. Other reactions may be to create flank brands that take off for price competition, while the other products are protected.

Phases and Reactions in a Price War

How you should react to a competitor's aggressive price competition depends on factors within the company, but also the environment [4]. Going straight onto the attack can be tempting, but not necessarily the smartest reaction. Figure 6.2, based on Nagle and Müller [4], shows four responses to a price competition.

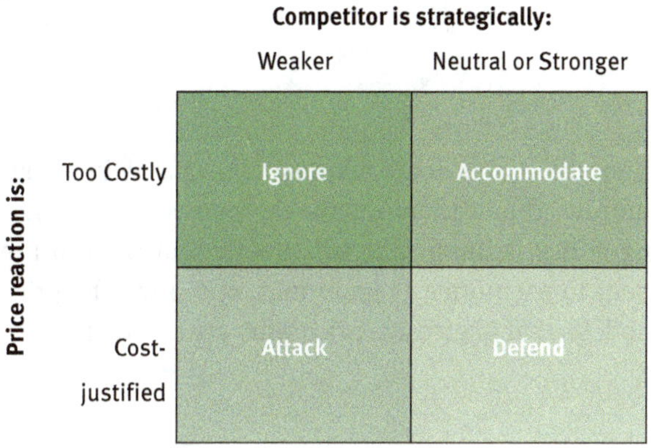

Competitor is strategically:

	Weaker	Neutral or Stronger
Too Costly	Ignore	Accommodate
Cost-justified	Attack	Defend

(Price reaction is:)

Figure 6.2: Responses to Price Competition [4].

Ignore

This reaction is correct when retaliation becomes too expensive. It is also correct if the competitor is so harmless that it has no intention to implement major initiatives. Moreover, large companies can survive low prices for a very long time, so you can use endurance tactics. Remember that if the goal is profit and not market share, an ignoring reaction will be correct. Often, it can be helpful to keep a weak competitor instead of opening up the opportunity for a new and stronger one.

Accommodate

When conducting an accommodation, you actively adjust your own competition strategy to minimize the damage caused by the competitor. At the same time, one is actively working to adapt to living under the new conditions. This is a defensive strategy to avoid price wars.

Attack

If you choose to go on the attack, this presupposes that the competitor is weaker, and that it will pay off in terms of cost to reduce the price. This reaction is chosen if you cannot "afford" to lose sales. If you choose such a reaction, a low-cost structure is required, so that you can survive the period. In the long run, this reaction will break small businesses.

Defend

If one chooses a defensive reaction, the goal is not to eliminate the competitors, but rather to convince them to withdraw. One wants to make the competitors understand that an aggressive pricing policy is financially unattractive for both in the long run. The signals that are sent to each other is important, and often the price reduction is only for a short period, so that aggressive price wars are avoided.

The Result of a Price War

When asking managers about who started the price war, 90 percent said it was the other company [30]. Many price wars start by accident. Even if a company lowers its prices, the intention is probably never to start an aggressive price war. Instead, competitors misinterpret their company's intentions and choose to respond aggressively [4]. One piece of advice is therefore to clearly communicate the intentions with the pricing policy, both internally within the company and externally to the competitors. Internal communication will make the company's employees work toward a common goal for the pricing policy. This means that the processing of price in the organization is implemented and carried out in a predetermined manner. If you choose to change the prices, it is advisable to pre-announce this to the market [4]. The competitors then know that the price reaction is for a specific time period or a specific product group and they can adjust their measures accordingly.

Leaders often misinterpret the outcome of a price war. They can loudly proclaim price reductions on hundreds of items. This is based on an expectation that demand will increase correspondingly, which offsets margins. In addition, they assume that as soon as one has won a new market share, is it OK to increase the prices. This is certainly not always the case as customers have established new reference prices against which they assess prices. Increasing the prices afterwards may prove impossible (see Figure 6.3).

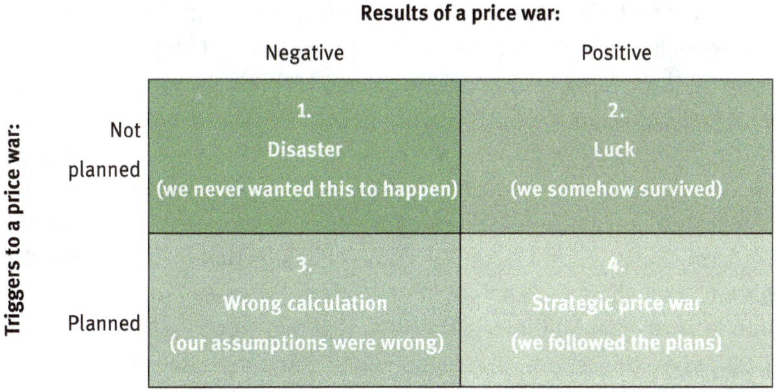

Results of a price war:

		Negative	Positive
	Not planned	**1.** Disaster (we never wanted this to happen)	**2.** Luck (we somehow survived)
	Planned	**3.** Wrong calculation (our assumptions were wrong)	**4.** Strategic price war (we followed the plans)

Triggers to a price war:

Figure 6.3: Triggers and the Result of a Price War.

How to Win a Price War

There are companies that want to go on a full frontal attack and start a price war. To succeed, there are several prerequisites that must be in place [4]. The first concerns the cost advantages. These must be larger than the competitors', either in the form of a flexible organization, different purchasing conditions, or cost advantages that the competitors cannot easily copy. In addition, one must have the financial backbone to bear the costs along the way.

A price war is also more likely to succeed if you are only looking for a small segment in the market, and you expect the competitors not to be willing to follow suit. Then you get to keep the newly acquired market shares for yourself. But price wars cost money. And for companies that can subsidize losses in one market through earnings in other, complementary markets will be better able to bear the costs. A final factor is if the price war leads to the total market increasing sufficiently so that the actual earnings are not reduced.

Price Wars in the Grocery Industry

A large study from the Dutch grocery trade mapped the long-standing effect of a major price war in the country [32]. The initiator of the price war was the market leader, who wanted to stop the leakage of market share to competitors.

The researchers found that the price war led to customers initially increasing trade as they spent more money on food. After the initial period, however, the size of each trade fell as customers changed their behavior to tactically buy products where they got the best price deals. The price war made customers price sensitive, and the effect of the weekly price changes became more important. The grocery chains that continued with the price war won customers during this period. The losers were the middle-class chains and the high-end players. Customers did not perceive any change in the pricing policy of these stores, and they lost the battle in the price awareness that had been created.

What did the chains achieve through the price war? First, those that started the price war won. The chain that started the price war achieved a positive price image without damaging the perception of their quality or their services. Those that followed did not report similar price effects. The second factor is that the initiator ended up with a higher market share than before the price war. Of course, the earnings did not demonstrate a corresponding increase, so the war had its costs. Thirdly, it was the chains that offered extra services and higher quality, and the chains in the middle layer, that lost from the war. Customers had been trained to be price sensitive and chose stores that ran hard discounts. The fourth effect of the price war, from the customers' point of view, was lower prices. This did not come without consequences. Lower margins as well as lower investments in product development, innovation, and research are detrimental to product quality and supply and will harm the consumer in the long run. The focus on service and selection is reduced. Fifth, not all chains will survive a price war, and bankruptcies will occur.

Recommendations for Grocery Chains

The study from the Netherlands provided the following advice to grocery chains regarding price wars [32]:

1. If the conditions of competition indicate that a price war is likely, it will pay to be first. The first man wins the attention of the customers.
2. High-end players should avoid using the price in their marketing. A price war will lead to customers becoming more price sensitive, and the stores are better served by investing in other customer segments.
3. The low-price chains have the advantage in price wars. They take advantage of their low prices and get customers' attention and thereby receive increased store visits. The low-price chains must lower their prices less than the middle-class chains to compete.
4. Managers should not be too overzealous even if a price war increases the influx of customers in the short term. In the long run, customers return to their original routines. But those who have an unattractive pricing policy risk losing customers forever.
5. The chains should study the customers' reactions before they step up a price war. If buying behavior changes only modestly or temporarily, it may be appropriate to compete on other marketing mix variables to win back customers. But if customer behavior changes significantly, you have little else to do but respond by reducing prices yourself.

6. The strongest wins. Where a price war is initiated by one of the leading chains, these will have the power and strength to stand out. They can cross-price finance the losses, they have negotiating power on their prices from the suppliers, and they still have most customers. If a price war is started by a chain in the middle layer, the chain can succumb on its own.
7. Price wars that are directed against competitors are less effective. Such competition aims to have cheaper shopping baskets than the competition. A better strategy is to focus on customer savings.

It is important to be aware of using the term "price wars" versus "price competition." Not every price cut is a price war. A price war goes much further than an ordinary price competition. The best vaccine against a negative price spiral is to focus on customer values and products' unique attributes, to communicate intentions with price politics clearly both internally and externally, as well as getting a good night's sleep before you set out the response to a competitor's aggressive pricing competition.

Summary

Few companies or customers are winners of a price war. Price wars can change the balance of power in a market and can result in near monopoly power and increased prices in the long run. In this chapter, I have described how a company should react if it is exposed to aggressive price competition that ends in a price war. The chapter also deals with possible outcomes of price wars as well as what must be in place to be able to win a price war at all. The chapter concludes with a description of research on price wars in the grocery industry.

Chapter 7
Unfair Price!

Introduction

Few things provoke customers more than if they feel they have been cheated on prices. This chapter is about customers' perceptions of unfair prices. The chapter starts with a step-by-step model for how companies can prevent and deal with consumers who perceive that they have received unfair prices. The chapter then goes through policies and legislation within marketing and price fixing.

It is appropriate to remind ourselves that all price variation that exploits customers' weaknesses or in some way tries to manipulate the customer negatively is a shortcut out of business. You fool a customer only once, and then the customer is gone forever.

Throughout this book, I recommend dynamic pricing, where you vary the prices based on the customers' willingness to pay. In Chapter 4 regarding different prices for the same product, I described how to vary the prices for the same product or service, while in Chapter 5 regarding different prices to the same customers, I wrote about how to get the same customer to voluntarily pay more for a product. In Chapter 9 on "psychological pricing," I even describe how a number of tricks can make products appear like a good buy, based on the way prices are presented. The message in this chapter is to vary prices based on the customer's premises.

Steps in Dealing with Unfair Prices

An indisputable premise is that all price variations must be perceived as fair by customers. Unfair treatment evokes in customers everything from anger to the desire to harm the provider in one way or another. This is also the reason why one should be very aware of whether customers perceive the criteria for price variation as fair. This means that customers must *qualify* for a lower price. This way the customers will not feel punished. Even giants like Coca-Cola make mistakes in their price discrimination. In one case they tried to vary prices on Coca-Cola vending machines based on air temperature. The logic was that hot weather would lead to a higher willingness to pay for the soda than on days with cooler weather. This was a short-lived experiment. Customers felt that they were being exploited, and the reactions were not long in coming.

In 2017, Richard Thaler [33] received the Nobel Memorial Prize in Economics for his research on human behavior in economics. His research includes the notion of justice. He and his co-authors found that customers place great emphasis on the reason for a price increase for this to be perceived as fair. Reasons that lie outside the

https://doi.org/10.1515/9783110987102-007

company's control were accepted, for example higher oil prices for the airline industry, while internal reasons are unacceptable. Examples include increased wages because of strikes. We will use this knowledge further when we discuss the framework for how to handle customers' perceptions of unfair prices (see Figure 7.1).

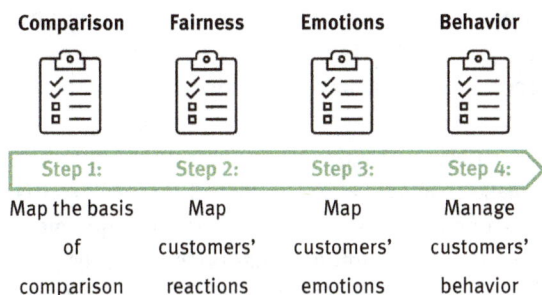

Comparison	Fairness	Emotions	Behavior
Step 1:	Step 2:	Step 3:	Step 4:
Map the basis of comparison	Map customers' reactions	Map customers' emotions	Manage customers' behavior

Figure 7.1: Steps in Dealing with Unfair Prices.

Step 1: Map the Basis of Comparison

Customers react differently to identical prices. If there are new customers in a market, they might not know how this market works and may react more strongly to price variation than customers with market experience. Customers with repeated transactions may therefore have a better understanding of why prices vary.

There is also a learning effect that affects customers' understanding and reactions to price changes. Research by Busse et al., [5] shows that sellers treat customers differently based on how well informed they give the impression of being. Researchers tested the assertion through car repair shops and found that the given prices varied according to the extent to which the customers perceived they were informed, uninformed, or misinformed about the market. When the customers assumed a price that was higher than the market price itself, the sellers followed up by offering a higher price, and the prices varied between women and men [5].

Yield management for flights has led to customers being accustomed to large price variations, and price-conscious customers plan accordingly. Also, the hotel industry implements such a pricing strategy. In its early stages it was perceived as unfair, but it has gradually become a more accepted industry standard. In addition, customers with a long-lasting relationship with a business or with a higher degree of confidence in it do not want to exploit their relationship. Such loyal customers can therefore withstand a higher degree of price fluctuations, without suspecting that they will be exploited. On the other hand, when customers see that the company is taking advantage of a situation by pushing the prices up in the short term, the reactions come quickly. A current example is the explosion in the prices of infection control equipment during the coronavirus pandemic.

What customers do not easily accept, however, are costs that the company itself has incurred, and which they try to transfer to customers [34]. I mentioned salaries earlier, while other examples include increased interest costs due to low liquidity, increased administration and document fees, parachutes for managers, more hirings, etc. Cost transfer from one group to another is perceived as unfair. Customers accept costs that the company cannot control. Examples include oil prices, US dollar exchange rates, new EU regulations that increase costs, higher electricity costs, etc. Companies deliberately use this when raising prices. In the event of increased air fares, we usually see a press release in advance where the airline specifies that the reason for the price increase is beyond their control. A recent major meta-analysis of research in the area supports the assumption that price increases justified by cost increases increase the perception of fair prices, while price increases that are not justified reduce the perception of fairness [35].

The final element in the basis of comparison is the degree of similarity between products and services [34]. By introducing some variation in the products, the customers will find that this is the reason for the price variation. This can be variation related to product attributes, service level, or quality. Companies use this deliberately through their branding policies. Examples include petrol stations that vary their prices based on whether the station provides car services, as well as different gasoline prices at different times of the week and during the day. These are variations that customers are both used to and accept. Price variation on charging electric cars, on the other hand, has not been incorporated into the market. While some charge per KWt, others charge for a combination of KWt and the number of charging minutes and provide a reduction in the subscription scheme. The lack of a common payment model for suppliers of various fast chargers makes the market unpredictable for the customer. Unpredictability again gives a perception of unfairness.

Step 2: Map Customers' Reactions

It is important to note that customers do not see justice and injustice as direct opposites. Customers make three evaluations: whether the prices are the same, whether the prices are different to the buyer's advantage, or whether the prices are different to the buyer's disadvantage. If the customer gets a better price than others, they see this as fair and something they likely have deserved. The reason is that customers want to maximize their own dividends. This is a result of their own merits and is in their own interest. When the evaluation is of the buyer's disadvantage, they are completely innocent. If they have paid a higher price than others, it is the company's fault, and the reactions lead to various emotions [34]. The theoretical reasoning for this type of reaction can be found in the attribution theory, which describes how people explain causal relationships.

The comparison customers make can be both explicit and implicit. Explicit comparison is when you compare prices directly against each other. Implicit comparison is when customers receive a higher price than they expected. The latter often happens when you enter into agreements on subscriptions, but find that the final price is much higher than you initially expected.

Moreover, research shows that if customers assume (although they do not know for sure) that a company charges unreasonably high prices in relation to their own costs, they choose this company's products. Some companies exploit this by signaling that they have higher costs than they do, and thus affect customers' cost/benefit perception [36]. In addition, customers consider large and strong companies to be less fair. This is because they assume that these companies will leverage their market power through controlling others and utilizing power through increasing prices [37].

Step 3: Map your Customers' Emotions

Customers who are exposed to what they perceive as unfair prices react cognitively and affectively [34]. The cognitive reaction, being the rational perception of price differences, affects customer satisfaction, future purchase intentions, and the motivation to complain. The affective reactions can vary in strength, from slight irritation to strong frustration. Perceived value is an assessment of how much one has sacrificed versus what one achieves from the benefits. The experience of having paid too much, therefore, leads to a reduced perceived value from the transaction, even if the product's attributes are the same. Thus, we also see that price-conscious customers will have a stronger reaction than customers for whom price is not that important.

Customers with a cognitive reaction often want to protect themselves financially by demanding financial compensation. Affective customers, on the other hand, may want to obtain both financial and psychological compensation.

In a *no-reaction* situation, the customer considers how much time, energy, and replacement cost it will entail to complete the purchase. For an Internet subscription, this includes the replacement of routers, passwords, payment agreements, etc. With a high threshold, the customers might choose to continue the agreement despite the fact that in principle they are dissatisfied. At the same time, these customers can hurt the company's reputation by spreading their dissatisfaction among friends and on social media.

Self-protection occurs when customers perceive an injustice to be so serious that they cannot accept it. Such customers complain, request a refund, spread negative rumors, and leave the relationship if possible. These customers will also put extra effort into finding alternative products or suppliers as well as identifying the costs associated with switching. The trade-offs are calculative, and customers leave the relationship if this benefits them.

The desire for revenge refers to customers with strong emotional reactions. These customers can be furious, angry, and rebellious. Ordinary conversations to discuss the situation can be difficult or impossible. Customers will achieve justice at whatever cost. They are happy to switch to the nearest competitor, even if this entails an even worse financial agreement than the original one. However, the psychological gain outweighs the feeling of loss. This type of customer is also inclined to contact nationwide media to make the injustice known to the whole world and beyond.

Step 4: Manage Customer Behavior

Damage control is best done preventively! Honest and fair pricing practices prevent situations with angry customers.

When a customer's dissatisfaction is based on an actual price difference, the best and simplest solution is to compensate them with a sum of money, give some form of reward, or give other forms of compensation. Thus, one accepts that the price discrimination was unfortunate, and gives the customer support in his or her view. This can lead to the customer having an even stronger bond with the company and finding that the company wants to act fairly.

If customers' reactions have a strong affective character, financial compensation will not always be sufficient [34]. Customers need just as much to vent their frustration. The goal must be for customers to express their frustration with the company rather than on social media. This gives the company the opportunity to explain why the situation has arisen, as well as to offer compensation. Listening to customers may remove the desire for revenge. It may even succeed in stopping customers having external damaging effects.

Pricing Marketing Guidelines

In the US, the Federal Trade Commission (FTC) organizes the Bureau of Consumer Protection (see https://www.ftc.gov/about-ftc/bureaus-offices/bureau-consumer-protection). Their mission is to stop unfair, deceptive, and fraudulent business practices. The FTC's guidelines on advertising and marketing (see https://www.ftc.gov/tips-advice/business-center/advertising-and-marketing) describe the regulations in the US for both brick and mortar and online sales.

In 2020, the European Commission drafted a new Consumer Protection Cooperation (CPC) regulation. The main changes consist of faster reactions and increased attention to digital everyday life. The CPC ensures that price information, price labeling, and price marketing comply with laws. European national consumer agencies have the authority to stop the marketing of products as well as impose fees and coercive fines for violations (see https://www.ccpc.ie/consumers/shopping/pric ing/rules-on-pricing/ and https://ec.europa.eu/info/law/law-topic/consumer-pro tection-law/unfair-commercial-practices-law_en).

The main points in the EU guidelines, which also make sense for other countries, on price marketing are as follows:

–   *Price information must be correct.* This means that information about prices must be clear, unambiguous, and complete.
–   *It is the average consumer's opinion that counts.* In other words, it is not the company's own view of how prices are perceived that is decisive.
–   *The total prices must be stated in all contexts.* The total price is the complete price the customer must pay for the item/service. This includes all taxes to consumers.
–   *The full price must be stated in all price marketing.* In other words, it is not enough to state the total price in small print at the bottom.
–   *When there are marketing cost advantages it must be clear what the basis for these price advantages is.* The usual basis is pre-price, competitor price, or price after the campaign. The price advantage must be real. The use of terms such as "sale," "seasonal sale," "rebate," "on offer," "discount," "Now €", and the like creates a consumer's expectation of a higher prior price and one must therefore be able to document this.
–   *Pre-price must be real.* As a rule, the price must have been used in the period before the sale and the product *must have been sold* at the stated pre-price. It is also not allowed to promote a luring offer that is not real. The use of the term "introductory offer" requires the item not to have been in the portfolio before.
–   *Comparative price must be stated.* If you state a comparative price such as the indicative price, price after the campaign, list price, package offer, price at competitors or at price comparison sites, such as pricee.com or best-price.com, you must mark the actual price and date of the comparison.
–   *The use of terms such as "cheapest," "lowest price," and the like must be documented in advance.* Expressions such as "I believe," "we mean," or similar statements do not exempt a company from the documentation obligation.
–   *The use of terms such as "price guarantee" must be documented.* This also applies to concepts such as price promise, low-price promise, and the like. The term "price guarantee" cannot be used if there are restrictions that make the right to a price guarantee unrealistic.
–   *The terms of the price match must be clear and unambiguous.* The time period must be emphasized, and the requirements for disclosure of evidence from the front user must not be unreasonable. Ad clips are enough.
–   *Free claims must be met.* When using the term "free" it cannot be added to fees, shipping, or other costs.

- The term "cheap" must only be used if performance of the same quality costs less than that of competitors. This includes imprecise terms such as "low-price profile," "low prices," and the like.
- Customer statements about savings such as "best," "cheapest," and so on must be documented. This also applies to editorial coverage in their own marketing.
- The use of terms such as "outlet," "factory sales," "stock sales," and "bankruptcy sales" must document in the usual way that the price difference is real. The terms can only be used if the prices are particularly lower than the prices at ordinary dealers.
- *The term "finance package" or equivalent must be real.* If it does not pay for the consumer to buy large packages, it is misleading to use such terms.

Guidelines for Price Cooperation

National competition authorities ensure that there is the best possible competition in all markets. National audits ensure that companies do not illegally cooperate with competitors on prices, division of markets, and restrictions on production or sales. In the US, the Clayton Antitrust Act and the Robinson-Patman Act are laws that exist to prevent anticompetitive price segmentation. Collusion goes under the term "cartel" and implies that all or part of the market is put out of play. It is a company's own responsibility to ensure that it does not enter illegal collaborations. The competition authorities handle applications for exemption from price cooperation.

Price collusion is illegal. A company cannot have contact with current or potential competitors regarding which prices to operate with.

Market sharing is illegal. A company may not have contact with current or potential competitors to divide customers or areas among themselves, set quotas, or agree on product specialization.

Tender cooperation is illegal. A company cannot cooperate on the submission of tenders, neither on price nor terms, before the tender is submitted.

Ethics and Legislation

Well-functioning and competitive markets are based on the premise that all transactions are voluntary. Ethical assessments for pricing strategies can be summarized in five points [4] (see Table 7.1).

Point 4 is especially interesting during the coronavirus pandemic, where we see that the prices of medical materials, such as antibacterial lotion and face masks, have shot up. Hand sanitizer comes in many sizes. Numbers from the Nielsen analysis bureau in the US show that the prices of hand sanitizer rose by 53% during the pandemic [30]. Network players that mediate such sales, such as Amazon.com, banned early on artificially high prices that exploit people in vulnerable situations.

Table 7.1: Ethical Criteria for Pricing.

Ethical criteria's	Implications
The price is paid voluntary	Customers shall be aware of the actual price of the product
The transactions are based on equal information	No information is kept hidden from exploited customer groups
No one shall exploit buyers voluntarily	The prices shall not exclude important customer groups from buying the products, such as medication
The prices are justified by costs	No prices shall vary based on exploiting the market, such as a shortage on products
The prices provide equal access to products	No transaction shall be based on personal gain

Summary

Dynamic pricing must be performed in a way that customers perceive as fair. This chapter started with a step-by-step model that shows how companies can prevent and deal with consumers who perceive that they have received unfair prices. The chapter then reviewed guidelines and legislation within price marketing and price cooperation.

Chapter 8
Price Tactics, Sales and Promotions

Introduction

While price tactics is the daily execution of price management in a company, pricing strategy is about the overarching rules you must follow. If these two are not developed in relation to each other, the actual pricing tactics can have a major devastating effect on the long-term pricing strategy. In this chapter, I will go through several ways to operationally work daily with prices. The chapter starts with a practical step-by-step framework for working systematically with tactical pricing decisions. Then I describe a whole range of different price promotions that are available. It is important to be aware that choices about the use of different price promotions have long-term consequences for what customers perceive as a fair price of a product. Arbitrary upward or downward adjustment of prices can therefore lead to long-term damage to sales. Therefore, if the work of price promotion exercises is not based on an established price strategy, the price execution might be completely arbitrary. This can lead to great harm to the company's long-term earnings.

Price promotions can be *proactive* when you want to expand a market, you want to increase sales or profits, or to develop customer advantages that provide superior performance to customers. Price promotions can also be *reactive*, such as in one's response to competitors' actions, to get rid of excess inventory, to increase short-term income, or to exit a product group or lay down the company.

Steps to Determine Tactical Pricing

Price promotions influence customers' expectations. Recent research by Shaddy and Lee [38] shows that price promotions cause customers to be more impatient because of the desire for quick reward [38]. This impatience triggers a higher willingness to pay to have a shorter waiting time. In this chapter the message is therefore that a primary goal of the price promotion is to get customers to make the purchasing decision *faster* than they would otherwise have done.

The following five steps (see Figure 8.1) are important decision criteria for implementing a price promotion [6].

https://doi.org/10.1515/9783110987102-008

Why	When	How much	How	Explain

Step 1:	Step 2:	Step 3:	Step 4:	Step 5:
The goal of	The time of	The size of	The execution	The
the price	the price	the price	of the price	communication
change	change	change	change	of the price
				change

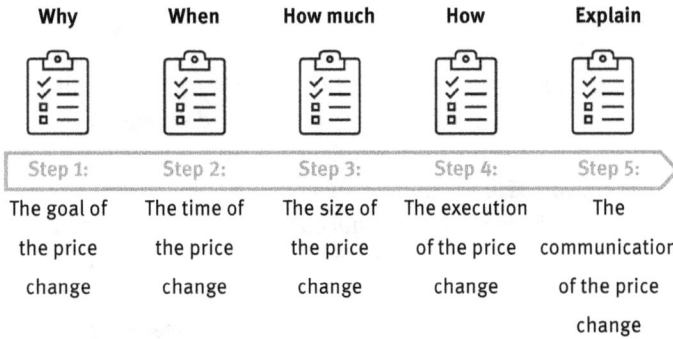

Figure 8.1: Steps for Determining Tactical Pricing.

Step 1: The Goal of the Price Change

The company must start by asking itself whether it really wants to use a price promotion. This question seems unnecessary but is essential for one to be aware of the strategic reason why one chooses to use a price promotion. Do you want to increase attention, increase sales, attract new customers, create incentives to change brand, or create loyal customers? Some customers carefully compare different products, while others shop out of sheer habit. Some customers may be very price conscious, while others are more brand loyal. Others want extra service and security for their purchases.

Next, you must decide who will be offered the price promotion. One must decide if it is directly to the customers, the distributors, or the retailers. If you choose one of the links in between, you must consider whether these allow a share or the entire price reduction to be passed on to the customers or not. Will the price promotion target the right customer segment? Sales can lead to changed associations among customers, such as perceptions of lower quality.

Step 2: The Time of the Price Change

When will the price promotion apply from? Is it for certain seasonal fluctuations? In response to competitor games? In case of sales failure?

How often should you have a price promotion? If you have price promotions too often, this could have a great impact on customers' willingness and expectations about the next sales period. Maybe they expect to never buy the product at full price.

How long should you have a price promotion for? At long intervals, it will be difficult to measure the real effect of the price promotion. In addition, this is an important signal to competitors, so that they know whether a price war is underway or not.

Step 3: The Size of the Price Change

How much should be offered in a price promotion? Do you have a special edition of a product to be sold in a certain quantity? Has the number been determined?

Which product variants should be offered for price promotion? Is it all versions within a product, or is it a specific size, edition, or specific models?

How and by how much should the price be reduced? The amount to be reduced must be determined, as well as the way it is to be done. This is also based on customers' price sensitivity and assumed reaction patterns.

How will the competitors react? Will they put down their prices correspondingly or even more? If so, how will we follow up on our price promotion?

The financial consequences of the price change must be calculated. How will cost promotion affect the sales and profitability of the business in the short and long term? Increased short-term sales may mean a shift in future sales, but at a lower price. In addition, the sales might affect targeted customers who are not willing to make cross-purchases of second products.

Step 4: The Execution of the Price Change

Price promotion is not just a percentage reduction in price. There are several different ways to make price promotions, ranging from price reductions, discounts, coupons, and codes to bonus programs and loyalty points. Research shows, among other things, that if the price reduction is compared with the sales price, customers perceive the price reduction as much larger than if it is compared with the original price [39].

Step 5: Communication of the Price Change

Make sure that the prices and price promotions that are communicated are easy to understand, transparent, and easy to handle internally [40]. Provide clear and practical information about what the offers entail. Provide true information about before and after prices. Avoid vague wording, such as "up to 50 percent discount." Reduce the time and energy it takes for a customer to take advantage of the offer. Registrations and filling in information reduce the effect. Avoid the term "suggested list price." Customers feel exploited. If the term "free" is used. Rather, you should tell them how much money it is about. For temporary price reductions, be precise about the start and stop date. Be clear about the actual cost incurred after an introductory offer on subscriptions.

Price Promotions

Price promotions may vary in time, product bundling, discounts on prices, and other factors.

Examples of different types of price promotions include:

1. early bid: buy before May 1, get a 50 percent discount on the price
2. last chance: buy now for 60 percent off, travel within 30 days
3. product bundling: get one free hotel night when buying a season ticket
4. 40 percent price reduction on the entire range
5. 10 percent discount on purchases over $100
6. free shipping
7. free sample pack
8. bonus packs, get more on the purchase
9. buy one, get one for free
10. buy one, get half price on the next
11. buy two, get the cheapest for free
12. three for two
13. seasonal discount
14. loyalty card
15. price match and price guarantees
16. free gifts
17. refund
18. $40 discount on the price
19. $1 market
20. reduced price: before $199, now $190
21. quantity discount: buy five get 5 percent discount
22. 1 percent discount per year in age
23. loyalty program
24. price packages
25. shelf price discount
26. coupons and digital codes
27. price cut: new price $19.90
28. bonus points
29. shock sellers
30. event and trade fair prices
31. industry-specific prices

Price Reduction

Reducing the price is the easiest factor to adjust, but this is also the situation for the company's competitors. Therefore, price reductions should be based on certain criteria that the customer must *meet to* access the discount. Remember that criteria used to discriminate against customers must be perceived as fair.

Time factors are widely used in price reductions: for example, that an item is sold with a price reduction for a certain *number of days*. Such a price reduction is often advertised continuously, so that customers are motivated to follow up and kept informed about what is happening in the companies. Another time factor is *seasons*, and everyone is used to seasonal sales after winter, summer, and holidays. Such seasonality has, however, tended to expand, so that you now have both pre-holiday sales and midsummer sales. The effect is that lower prices are expected throughout the year. We also see more and more businesses using *holidays and anniversaries* as a price variation factor: for example, having Singles Day/Week and Black Friday phenomena increased, as well as sliding into Black Week (see Figure 8.2). Countries like the US tend to combine sales and various anniversaries – everything from Presidents' Day to Veterans' Day, etc. Remember, however, that such a sale is not necessarily appropriate. If a price reduction gives less income than in ordinary activities, the purpose must be reconsidered. Recent research shows that price promotions around major events, such as the Olympics, generate higher sales only if one is careful regarding the choice of synergy between brands and the events [41]. *Expiration date* is a time factor that is used more and more. Instead of grocery stores throwing away products that are close to expiration, they sell them at greatly reduced prices a few days before the date expires. Such a strategy both appeals to a sustainability perspective with less food waste and is available for all customers who have a desire for green consumption [42]. The majority of customers who shop for these types of products are also customers at other food stores.

Figure 8.2: Black Friday All Week.

The advantage of using price reductions as a tactic is that they motivate customers to shop for products earlier or shop for products they otherwise would not have done. Customers are often more concerned with how much they save, rather than how much they spend. And customers perception of a good deal results in satisfied customers. Also, if the purchase is made under a time limit, i.e., "run and buy purchases" before they are sold out, customers also feel that they have accomplished something that rewards themselves. Using different social media, you can now differentiate to a much greater extent the customer groups, so that you can target the tactics at specific customer groups that you want to reach. This can be new customers or other types of customers, or making existing customers aware of new usage opportunities. In addition, it can be a reminder to existing customers to come back and use the business more often, and thus try to increase customer loyalty. The risk of using price reductions is when it is done without goals or purpose. If you engage in a wave completely reactively, such a tactic can result in large loss of income. And if you offer the wrong products, customers will quickly understand that they are being exploited. This comes back to strike you. Price reductions that are used too often also destroy the basis for ordinary prices.

Discounts, Codes, and Coupons

A discount is something that is given back at a paid price. This can be in the form of percentages, a $ amount, or as a refund and the use of coupons. One example is that with a trade you get a coupon with a 10 percent discount on the next purchase if it is used within a certain time. Online stores often have specific codes with limited duration that one needs to enter to obtain discounts. Another type of discount is a percentage off on the next trade if you recommend the website to a friend.

The decision on which products should be given a discount or not must be seen in connection with complementary and substitute products. A complementary product is a product that is purchased together with the main product, such as a PlayStation and games. A substitute product is a product that can replace the main product, such as Netflix and HBO Max. Cross-price elasticity – that is, how the sale of one product affects the sale of another – affects whether a discount obtains the desired effect. If a 10 percent discount on the sale of a PlayStation increases the sale of games by 20 percent, the discount can lead to increased profit. However, if the discount on Pepsi Max soda only increases the sales of this soda, you must calculate how much extra you must sell in order not to lose profit. Elementary techniques for calculations are described in Chapter 12 on pricing calculations.

The advantages and disadvantages of discounts follow the same discussion as for price reductions. The effect of discounts can be even more targeted when the customer receives them physically as part of the receipt. For online shopping, codes, which are in fact a type of digital coupon, can be used purposefully to get customers to complete a trade on items they have left behind in the shopping cart. At other times it can be used as a reward: for example, you get a code for a discount on your birthday or when the company has a birthday. However, some customers become coupon experts, and large purchases with the deliberate use of coupons can be a real loss for the business. Through conscious use of media channels, coupons can provide targeted measures to specific demographic customer groups. Another advantage is that you get attention even though many customers forget to use the coupons when buying. However, if you make coupons with too strong restrictions, such as a very short deadline, this can hurt rather than promote the company's reputation [43].

Price Bundling

Price bundling is a well-known phenomenon. Buy two, get the cheapest for free! Or three for the price of one! Customers perceive that they get more than they pay for and experience this as a good deal. Methods for product bundling are well described in Chapter 4 on different prices for the same product and include price as a mechanism.

The advantage of price bundling is that you do not harm the reference price. Customers will receive incentives to shop for more money than they otherwise would have done, and the total sales increase. However, it is important that the products that are chosen provide extra value to the customers. If you combine the wrong products in a price bundle, the irritation can outweigh the expected increase in value. Again, it is about understanding the customer and creating a product mix that builds on their premises.

Loss Leader

A loss leader is a product that is sold below market price and sometimes also below production price. The purpose of a loss leader is to capture the attention and draw customers into the store or to the website. The goal is then to sell other products that offset the loss. A loss leader must be a product with a high degree of price sensitivity so that the price reduction affects the buying behavior. A classic example is an extraordinarily cheap turkey for thanksgiving (see Figure 8.3).

The advantage of using a loss leader is that you can remind previous customers to return to the store and get the attention of new customers. Grocery stores often use loss leaders to signal that they want customers through reduced prices, and they use the tactic deliberately as a marketing effort. Customers understand, of course, that this is a game and is used only when it suits them. In addition, there is a risk of products being sold out, and the whole effect might become negative. Moreover, if the loss leader attracts customers who do not want to spend more money in the store, the whole tactic fails. Another unsuccessful strategy is to create a loss leader based on surplus stock. Such surplus stocks are based on the corporate

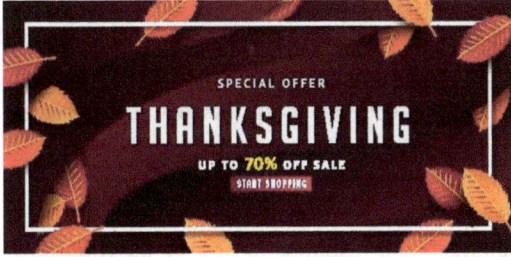

Figure 8.3: Season sales.

or the store's premises and not the customers' needs. The effect may therefore be absent. The reputational effect of a failed loss leader can also be more damaging than if one did not choose such a tactic.

Loyalty Programs

The purpose of loyalty programs is to get ordinary customers to become permanent customers with repurchases. Loyalty programs use different strategies. The most common are bonus points for each purchase, where you collect points and can turn these into items or other reward systems. Loyalty programs were formerly used widely in the grocery and airline industries, and these have now expanded into coffee shops, clothing stores, and online shopping. Everyone now asks for a mobile number with a view to including the customer in the customer club.

The advantage of a loyalty program is that, when done properly, it gets the customer to feel appreciated. Satisfied customers return and become loyal. The loyalty program is thus used as a differentiating element to separate the store from the competing stores. At the same time, as more and more loyalty programs are being offered, the actual distinction between them becomes more difficult to maintain. The value of the data and the ability to segment customers based on various criteria have been important effects of a loyalty program. However, customers have become more concerned about how data on their personal purchasing behavior are disseminated and used. The European General Data Protection Regulation (abbreviated to GDPR) has set a completely new standard for how shops and companies can collect and use this type of data. Consent is required and makes the work with the loyalty programs far more demanding. The US government has not implemented corresponding regulations. However, it is important to note that the GDPR applies to organizations operating within the EU and those worldwide that target – directly or indirectly – individuals in the EU.

Adaptation of Price Tactics According to Customer Value

There are several recurring mistakes that businesses make in connection with pricing tactics. These are often the result of ill-considered plans and result in incorrect effects of the price promotion [6].

1. Price reductions within the seasons are often unprofitable.
2. Price reductions too often reduce customers' willingness to pay.
3. Price reductions often have little effect as a response to new competing brand launches, product packages, or innovations.
4. Price reductions are more effective when you launch your own new brands.
5. Price reductions do not fix a bad product.

Price tactics are all about creating boundaries and separation that ensure that customers must qualify for a price reduction. A healthy price tactic works dynamically with prices so that they are constantly optimal for the various customer segments' willingness to pay. If the price is too high in relation to a customer segment's willingness to pay, it will be a missed opportunity. And vice versa, if the prices are set too low, they will be unused opportunities (see Figure 8.4).

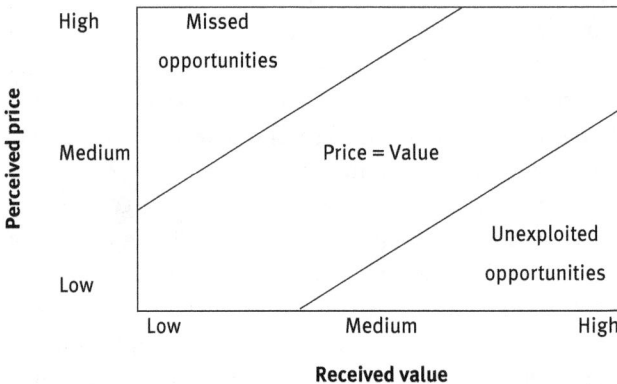

Figure 8.4: Adjust the Price Points According to Value.

Missed opportunities are markets where the product has been overpriced in relation to the customers' perceived value. What often happens in such cases is that the company assesses the product according to its own value, not the customer's opinion. In such cases, it is easy to imagine that the only solution is to reduce the price. But the problem is just as often that one has not been able to identify the factors that create value for the customer.

One example of this is the newspaper industry, which due to the transition to digital newspapers is struggling to get paying customers. They try everything from free weeks, to $5 for five weeks, to giving customers access to three free articles per week. Nothing seems to work. Despite the initiatives, customers have a low willingness to pay. What is interesting is that the various papers think of each other as competing products (substitutes), while customers see them as complementary. Often, customers want cases covered from different geographical areas, with different opinions, and with different journalists. The Amedia media company realized this by understanding that a reader is not only interested in a single newspaper, but a combination of newspapers. They therefore combined their subscription scheme to include all 73 national and local newspapers. As a result, they experienced a 43% increase in paying subscriptions.

Price Guarantees

Price guarantees are about a company guaranteeing to pay the difference if customers find the same product at lower prices elsewhere. This makes it easier for companies to market their price-match guarantees rather than their actual prices. Customers, therefore, associate the business with low prices, without necessarily knowing the exact prices.

New research shows a paradox within price guarantees in that customers assume that this type of store offers the lowest prices [44]. Customers who have large search costs would therefore prefer to shop at these vendors rather than spending time searching for the lowest prices in the market. The irony is that this means that companies can charge higher prices than they would have done without such a price guarantee in the market.

Summary

Tactical pricing, or "price promotions" as it is also called, has a great effect on a company's long-term earnings. In this chapter, I have gone through several ways to work operationally with prices daily. The chapter started with a practical step-by-step framework for working systematically with tactical pricing decisions. After that, I reviewed a whole range of available price promotions.

Chapter 9
Pricing Psychology

Introduction

In this chapter, I show how the individual perception of a price, payment, or discount is affected both by the number itself and by the visualization, the environment, and the way the price is combined with other prices. The chapter starts with a description of reference price and how customers focus on transaction benefits rather than the actual price they pay. Next, I give an example from an online booking site, where a whole range of techniques is described. Finally, I review four steps that describe the use of psychological pricing.

Most people are familiar with the use of 90, 95, and 99 endings. But did you know that if customers get the choice between "buy one, get one for free" and "two for 50 percent," most customers choose the first option? Even if the actual amount is the same, the first option is perceived as better. When we get one free on a purchase, this is seen as an additional value, while a discount of 50 percent is perceived as a reduced loss [45].

How Much You Save Is More Important Than How Much You Pay

This section should be called "transaction utility and acquisition utility" [46]. It's about the fact that customers are often more concerned about how much money they save on a trade (transaction utility) than about how much they pay (acquisition utility). To illustrate this, when we have been at a sale in a store, we come home and announce how much money we have saved! We seldom talk about how much money we have spent.

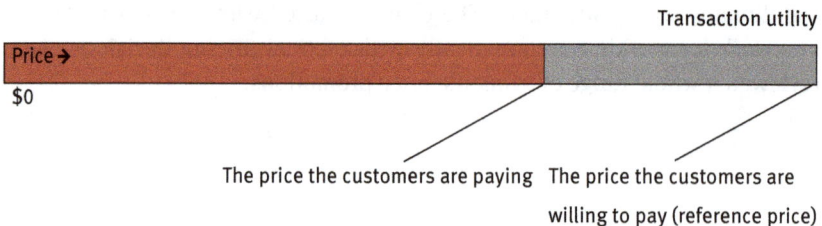

Transaction utility

Price →

$0

The price the customers are paying   The price the customers are willing to pay (reference price)

Figure 9.1: The Relationship between Transaction Utility and Acquisition Price.

This relationship is illustrated in Figure 9.1. It shows that customers have a reference price that sets the level for what they consider to be an acceptable price. If

https://doi.org/10.1515/9783110987102-009

they obtain a price that is lower, the trade is perceived as good, and they focus on the transaction utility. As mentioned earlier, the reference price, which is the willingness to pay, is affected by several factors, the most common of which are experience, the environment, and the numbers you are exposed to here and now.

Number Magic on e-Commerce Sites

Let's analyze a regular website that sells hotel accommodation (see Figure 9.2).

(1) Note that the list of hotels is sorted by featured hotels. In very small letters it states that the sorting order is based on the compensation the network operator receives from the hotels. In other words, the order is not trivial. However, often we do not look at the top of the screen when we start searching for a hotel. We turn our focus straight to the prices and selection of hotels.

(2) A Covid-19 restriction warning pops out in yellow color. Here one must fill in details about the country of residency, vaccination, and insurance to get information about travel restrictions and regulations.

(3) They deliberately include reviews from other guests. This is because it is difficult to evaluate the quality of experience with products before trying them. We, therefore, put extra trust in other customers' opinions.

(4) Let's then look at the actual price of the accommodation. The original price of $1,626 per night is detailed and includes the number 6. The accommodation has a special offer at $1,271 per night. Ergo, the last digit is now number 1, and we experience the cost as lower. In addition, the first numbers have gone from 16 to 12, which is perceived as a big reduction. Interestingly, when multiplying $1,271 by 7 nights, the total price is $8,897, while the total price is stated as $10,460. The stated total price is perceived as a good bargain since it consists of round numbers, while the actual total price requires the mental capacity to interpret and therefore is perceived as higher. And red prices? Well, as we will see in this chapter, they work well. The sizes of the letters affect which numbers we see first. And with a price of $10,460, we see the next option at $3,227 as a bargain (5). In other words, our reference price was strongly affected. It is not a coincidence that the first hotel on the list is more expensive than the second one.

Did you notice that the first and second hotels are marked with "Ad" and the third and fourth hotels are identical with identical prices (6)?

Bonus points are good and feel less painful to use (7). So, all the options here can collect bonus nights. Ergo, this can affect our choices.

Secret prices must be a deal in our favor (8)! But wait, by clicking on the link one must be a member to qualify for the offer. But this is urgent. The second alternative, which costs $3,227, and which now looks very attractive (and which also

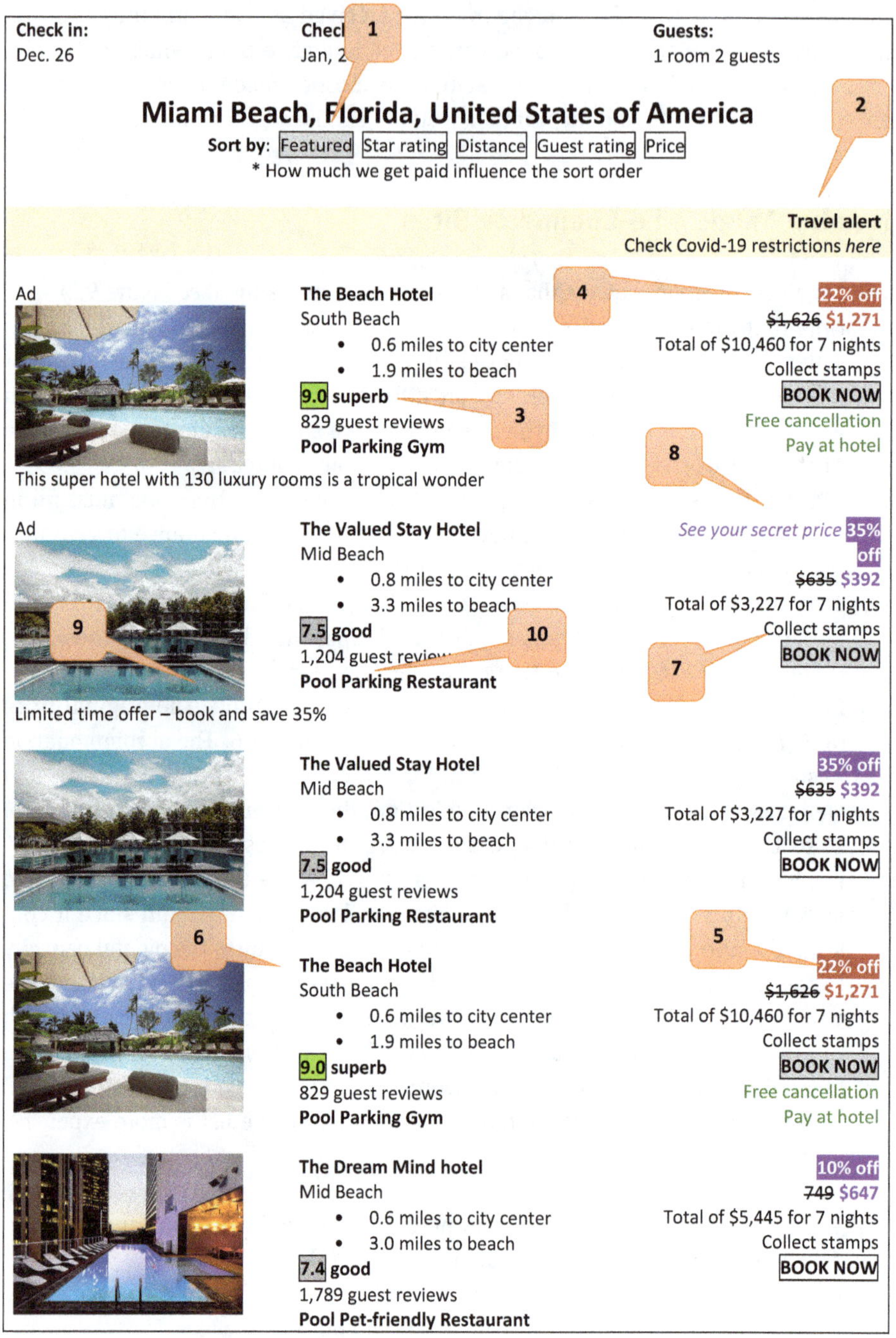

Figure 9.2: Illustration of Hotel Prices Online.

has a sponsored follow-up), has a limited-time offer of 35% savings [9]. Because this reservation is far into the future, we do not get the usual "sold out" option. As customers, this gives us no additional information when choosing among the alternatives. The reason why they include it is that we feel the time pressure and are reminded that as time passes the choices disappear.

So, the question is: what's the actual price (10)? A link that comes up only after you have clicked on one of the hotels says: "See fees and policies for additional details or extra charges." Therein lies the answer. A mandatory resort fee of $45 per day per room will be added. Parking is not included, even though the room costs $10,000. They charge $45 a day for parking. Do you have many children? This costs extra per day. Are you planning to bring your dog? This costs an extra one-time price of $150. And of course, international residents must not forget the 20 percent tip in the United States. By the way, fancy a balcony? Sea view? Extra fees. Breakfast? This depends on the choice you make. With some of the other hotel options there are also additional charges for getting access to the facilities (gym, swimming pool, etc.), Wi-Fi in public areas, early check-in, and so on.

Accordingly, even though we decided to go for the second choice with a price of $3,227, the realized price will be close to $4,430. The most expensive option on the first hotel for this period is stated as being US$10,460. This is admittedly exclusive of taxes. But then we are probably over in a customer segment where the price is insignificant, and that segment is hardly in the target group for this book, so we leave it at that.

Remember that all the world's psychological tricks cannot fix a bad, overpriced product to make it good. Deceiving a customer to make choices they could otherwise not have done hits back hard. You only fool a customer once. Then they, and everyone around them, are gone forever. And so it should be. Transparency and openness about what customers pay is the rule.

Steps in Psychological Pricing

As we have seen in the previous example, there are many ways to present prices, including which numbers to use, print size, color, comparisons, order, the time factor, shortages, and so on.

In this section, I will go through a whole series of such techniques and explain how they work. All techniques are based on research in reputable academic journals. The techniques are based on established theories within the information economy, and especially the theories around reference price effect, anchoring effect, prospect theory, and endowment effect.

Because this book has an applied purpose, I decide to focus on how the theories are applied. To simplify the process, I've organized it into four steps (see Figure 9.3).

These are Step 1, the choice of numbers; Step 2, map the surroundings of the numbers; Step 3, identify the motives for purchase; and Step 4, create a good trade.

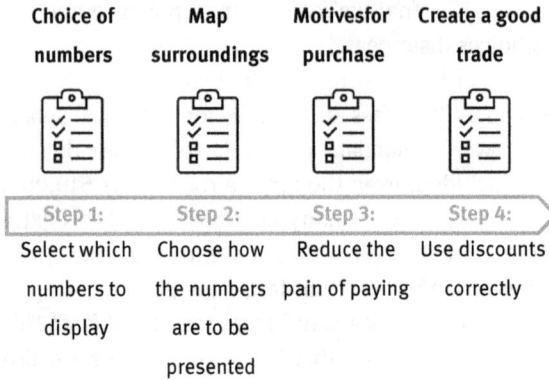

Choice of numbers	Map surroundings	Motivesfor purchase	Create a good trade
Step 1: Select which numbers to display	**Step 2:** Choose how the numbers are to be presented	**Step 3:** Reduce the pain of paying	**Step 4:** Use discounts correctly

Figure 9.3: Steps in Psychological Pricing.

Step 1: Select Which Numbers to Display

In this first step in psychological pricing, we will look at how numbers should be presented to customers. We will first look at the well-known 99 ending technique. Then we will look at how the way the numbers are presented influences the perception of whether the price is high or low. Are there complicated numbers? Sometimes it's an advantage, other times not. Which is better, whether a price goes up or down, right or left? Sometimes we accept numbers without reacting, while in other situations a price invites haggling. The techniques here may work a few times but other times not. The sample shows the variation and what the research has found so far. There are no absolutes.

The choice of number bases itself on the *reference price effect*. The reference price effect is about the internal standard with which you compare a specific price. If it is products you buy frequently, such as grocery products, you have much better knowledge about the prices of competing products in this category. If it is products you seldom buy, the price comparison is based more on expected price levels or historical prices. The research contribution on reference price has developed over the years. In the post-war years, the reference price was perceived as prices being compared against a subjective interval, and the larger the interval, the more uncertainty prevailed over the correct price. In the 1970s, one focused more attention on how much customers remembered previous prices [47]. Attention was focused on memory research and how customers perceived, coded, processed, stored, and recalled prices when making purchasing decisions. *Explicit* and *implicit memory* became important, and a distinction was made between remembering and knowing prices. Price psychological effects on the processing of numbers were emphasized, and, not least, how conceptual factors (Burger King advertising) and perceptual factors (hunger) recreate implicit price memories.

Cognitive capacity affects the perception of prices. Studies show that customers perceive round prices as more readily available, as it requires less cognitive capacity to perceive them. This affects purchases that have to do with habits [48]. An example where cognitive capacity comes into play is the number of syllables in the price. Our brain works all the time, regardless of our consciousness. Even though we do not stand in a store and say the numbers out loud to ourselves, the brain interprets it in this way when we read the prices. Research shows that prices with many syllables are perceived as higher [49]. A price reduction with fewer syllables is therefore perceived as a lower price: For example, (1,350) one-thous-and-three-hund-red-and-fif-ty has nine syllables, while (1,500) one-thous-and-five-hund-red has six syllables. Research has also tested the use of a comma to mark thousands in a price. And they found that if you removed the marking, customers perceived the prices as lower. Why? Because with a comma we read it as (1,350) one-thousand-three-hundred-and-fifty with a total of nine syllables. Without a comma we read it as (1350) thir-teen-fif-ty, that is, four syllables, and thus a perceived lower price [49].

Emotion affects the cognitive capacity. If you are selling products that appeal to emotions, such as makeup, training clothes in fresh colors, or crime novels, show numbers that are easy to process mentally. This gives a feeling of well-being and matches the product category. The opposite is also true. If you are about to sell protein powder to training fanatics, you must bear in mind that such individuals have put a lot of time and effort into finding the right formula, amount, and diet. Prices that require more cognitive processing will correspond to the category to which they belong. Complicated pricing will make the product feel right [50]. However, there is also research that has tested whether this effect really exists, and the conclusion is that it is weaker than previously claimed [51].

Specific numbers are perceived as honest. A study of attribute prices has investigated the difference between using round numbers and specific numbers in the ads. The researchers found that customers paid more when the numbers were stated specifically, such as 217,565 rather than 215,000 [52]. Customers in fact perceived the specific price to be lower, even though it was in fact higher. A specific price led to increased uncertainty as it did not fit with established practice. In addition, using specific numbers gives the impression that the price is determined through careful calculations and reflects the actual costs. This could have implications for how list prices can be used. In addition, the customers perceived round prices as an invitation to negotiate.

Experiments show that if you start negotiations with a precise number format, for example $746, the customer assumes that the actual amount is close to the price [53]. If, on the other hand, you start with $800, the customer will perceive the negotiation room as much larger. Specific numbers thus reduce the subjective perception of the scale on which prices vary (see Figure 9.4).

Round numbers	
Used car:	$ 14,500

Specific numbers	
Used car:	$ 14,578

Figure 9.4: Specific Figures at High Prices.

"*The power of 99*" is a well-known pricing technique. A price of 24.90 is perceived as much lower than 25.0. This is because we read the numbers from left to right, and 4 is lower than 5. In addition, numbers from 0 to 4 are considered low, while numbers from 6 to 9 are perceived as high. Therefore, 24.90 is a better option than 26.90 [54]. The irony is that a price of 34 is perceived as less attractive than a price of 39. By increasing the price by 5, the sale often increases.

In addition, we are trained to assume that extensions of 90, 95, or 99 indicate that the product is on sale. So these are good deals. Brand stores such as Ralph Laurent deliberately use the 99 extensions only on sales products, while they use round prices on ordinary products. This is to ensure that their clothes are not perceived as a cheap brand. However, be aware that the research on 99 effects reports mixed results.

Step 2: Choose How the Numbers are to be Presented

How big is a price change? This depends on what it is compared against. This comparison is not only about the numbers that are presented together, but also about how they are placed visually, their color, and the size of the letters. In these examples, taken from research, we will look at how various effects work.

Anchoring effect is about which number you consciously or unconsciously compare a price against. This theory shows that even a random number in the surrounding, whether related or not, influences the perception of whether a price is high or low. Customers unknowingly compare the price to the exposed number. Research shows that if a group of customers is given different temperatures – let's say one group is given 25 degrees Celsius, while another group is given 7 degrees Celsius – those with the highest temperature will pay significantly more for a product than those with the lower temperature [55]. The same effect is found when a poster with completely random numbers is hung on the wall.

When one customer has established an anchor that he or she compares the prices to, it is difficult to change the willingness to pay afterward. This is because changing your mind requires unlearning, acceptance of past mistakes, and the ability to accept new evidence. As a prerequisite to expose customers to previously higher prices for the same product, the previous prices must be based on facts and a true situation (see Chapter 7 regarding the price-communication regulations).

Showing a price reduction without referring to the previous price has no anchoring effect. This makes it more difficult for customers to assess the value of the discount. The interesting thing here is that you can expose customers to higher prices for *a second product*. Even in these cases, the reference price will be affected (see Figure 9.5).

Prices without exposure	
Backpacker:	$ 175

Prices with exposure	
Backpacker:	$ 175
We also sell the following hiking items:	
Wind jacket:	$ 350
GoreTex pants:	$ 310

Figure 9.5: Price Exposure.

The anchoring effect has a very strong impact on customers' reservation prices. A review of research on the anchoring effect demonstrates that mood and individual differences (ability, personality, and information styles) matter little for the anchoring effect [56].

The wording used on prices affects the perceived price. The use of words that describe a deal affects whether the prices are perceived as high or low. If we use the term "high" versus "low," this will prime (affect) the perception of whether the price is high or low [49]. The word "high" gives associations with a high price, and vice versa. If you are going to launch a new, expensive product, you will intuitively think that the old products should be reduced in price. However, this is not always correct. By lowering the price, you lower the reference price. One option is therefore to rather *increase* the price of the former products in the portfolio.

Similarly, small numbers are perceived as stronger. Changes in small numbers, i.e., numbers from 0 to 4, are perceived as more significant than endings in large numbers, i.e., numbers from 6 to 9. Therefore, a price reduction from 4 to 3 is perceived as stronger than a change from 8 to 7. Research shows, however, that this effect is reduced if there are more than three digits [57].

Visualization of the price exposure affects the price perception. Should prices be presented in specific colors? Research shows that it all depends on whether you are a man or a woman [58]. A price reduction that is shown in red has the greatest effect on men. The reason is said to be that men use visual symbols more actively, while women are generally more aware of prices when shopping and therefore are better at recalling previous prices. This also means that for products where there is a high degree of involvement the effect decreases.

The larger the letters, the larger we experience the prices to be. This is an advantage if you want to form a reference price for comparison. If, on the other hand, we want our own price to be perceived as low, a smaller font size will make the prices seem lower [49].

The order of the price exposure affects the perception of prices. Should you show the price or the product first? It all depends on what type of product it is and whether the customers are price sensitive. MRI scans (brain scan) show that if you are exposed to the price first, this affects the evaluation the most [59]. If you are exposed to the product first, the product becomes most important. For regular products it can therefore be best to display the price initially, as this is most likely to result in a purchase. This is because these customers are considering to a greater extent whether the product is worth it. Accordingly, when selling expensive luxury products, it would be more appropriate to display the product first. This is because the assessment of the customer is whether they like the product. The price is, therefore, less important as customers are not price sensitive for these kinds of purchases.

We all have mental maps in our mind that unconsciously control how we perceive an event. We finish our food, burn a candle, look up at the sky and down to hell, we look up at our football team, while we look down at our opponents. We also use direction when we read the numbers from 0 to 9: The lowest numbers are on the left, the highest on the right. This unconscious mental map affects the perception of prices. If we are going to make something look cheap, it should be placed to the left. When we want to make something look like good value, we place it on the right. And on websites, we place small numbers at the bottom of the page and high numbers at the top [60].

If you are in a sports store and are first exposed to a backpack at $98, another backpack at $125 will be perceived as expensive. On the other hand, if you are first introduced to a backpack at $295, a backpack at $125 is perceived as cheaper. The reason for this is that at low–high the reference price is formed based on the $90, while at high–low the reference price is formed from the $200 numbers.

Reading order has a significance for the numbers we see first. By placing the highest number on the left, this will be read first and shape the reference price. This applies to all numbers. A price change from $79 to $65 is perceived better than a price change from $82 to $68 (see Figure 9.6). Both have a price change of $14. The reason is that the change from 7 to 6 is perceived as smaller than the change from 8 to 6. And, not least, this change means that customers are now buying the most expensive alternative, at the same time as they consider the trade to be better.

Reading left numbers	
Hiking socs:	Was $7.90 Now $6.50
Hiking socs:	Was $8.20 Now $6.80

Figure 9.6: Numbers Are Read from Left to Right.

Step 3: Reduce the Pain of Paying

Paying for a product feels like sacrificing something. But the experience becomes less painful when we get more time. Also, it is better to pay small amounts today than large amounts in the future. Does a customer have a guilt feeling when buying your wellness products? Bundle them together with a functional benefit product and give them the right price reduction.

The prospect theory is based on the work by Kahneman, for which he received the Nobel Memorial Prize in Economics in 2002 [61]. The theory shows that losses and gains are perceived differently even if they are for the same amount of money. To explain the theory, imagine that you are about to contact a kennel to buy a small, lovely Australian Cobberdog puppy. You will then be asked if you want to buy pet insurance. Although these beautiful dogs are kind of a new breed, the puppy has strong, healthy parents. In other words, it will be difficult to predict whether the dog is going to be a big expense in the future. So, the question is whether you are willing to take a future risk with a possible high cost, or whether you will pay a smaller annual amount to hedge against a risk that may never come.

The prospect theory describes how people choose between different alternatives, and how they (often incorrectly) interpret the probability of future events. Customers want to avoid future losses, even when the probability is minimal. They are therefore more willing to accept a sure loss on the day. This variation in the value of loss or gain has had a major impact on pricing strategies, and several of the effects in this chapter show exactly how customers act irrationally due to risk aversion.

Language related to money increases the pain. If you see the $ sign next to a price, this reminds you of the pain of spending money. And this can lead to you wanting to pay less. The pain of paying can be triggered quite easily. In fact, the $ sign can lead people to use less money [62]. At the same time, the sign must sometimes be used for customers to understand that it is the price the number symbolizes. This tactic can therefore only be used where the customer is in no doubt that this is the price in question. One example is the prices on a restaurant menu, which are often displayed without the sign.

It feels less painful for a customer to use bonus points if these are called something other than money. For example, the United airline uses the term "MileagePlus" points, while the airline company Norwegian uses "CashPoints." According to the research, it will feel more painful to use Norwegian's points [63]. The more difficult it is for a customer to tie points to an actual amount of money, the easier it is for them to use their points. What do bonus points from loyalty cards and gift cards have in common? They both reduce the pain of paying. By distinguishing between means of payment and customers' own money, the perception of payment changes [63]. Of course, customers know they are paying, but it is easier to use this type of payment as it does not represent money out of the pocket. Also, the combination of bonus points and actual payment reduces the psychological cost of paying. The same effect is also seen if one compares the use of payment cards versus physical money. It is more painful to pay with physical money than to enter a code for the payment card.

Next, researchers recommend focusing on time rather than money when describing a product [64]. Time increases the awareness of the experience with the product, while money leads to a focus on the ownership of the product. The effect is assumed to be strongest for nonprestige products (see Figure 9.7).

Products with the price in focus	Products with time in focus
Our spa-treatment will give you value for money	You will appreciate the time you spend at our spa

Figure 9.7: Products Where the Focus Is on Money versus Time.

You have probably noticed it: Many products have much smaller packages now than before! And the potato chip bag now contains more air than potato chips. This is an effective way to avoid price increases. Reducing the packaging reduces costs and increases margins. And not least, it contributes to avoiding negative attention to price changes. If this takes place through small changes, it is not easily noticed either. Reducing the physical size of a product decreases the costs and increases margins. Even more important is the fact that increasing the income is achieved without raising the price (or warning people about a negative change). The changes can take place in four dimensions, namely the height, width, length, and weight of the product [65].

Customers care about the experienced size of the price (i.e., whether it is high or low). But they also care about the perceived fairness of the price. Even if the price is low, customers can still perceive the price as unfair. In the same way, customers may still perceive high prices as reasonable – depending on a few factors. Customers perceive cost-based pricing as fairer than prices based on market conditions [34]. But, because customers do not have knowledge about the company's costs or quality, the transparency increases buyers' perception of justice. An emphasis on the quality of the ingredients will be perceived to justify the price.

Bundle products with hedonistic benefits. There are many ways to bundle products. When it comes to willingness to pay for the various product bundles, research reports an effect when wrapping hedonistic benefits [22]. Hedonistic purchases are about immediate happiness, but often trigger guilt. This guilt is reduced when the product or service is bundled with a utilitarian product. The same research also shows that when one bundles hedonistic products together, price reduction has less effect than when bundling products across categories (see Figure 9.8).

Studies [22] also show that if two new products are bundled together, the bundle is perceived as more attractive if its delineation of one product in the bundle has a hedonistic approach. Example: The kitchen machine can be used to make exotic dishes (hedonistic) versus the kitchen machine can be used to make healthy dishes (utilitarian).

Bundling with ordinarily price reduction	
Kitchen tool and sentenced candle	Save $5

Bundling with hedonistic price reduction	
Kitchen tool and sentenced candle	Save $5 on the sentenced candle

Figure 9.8: Bundling Price Reduction on Hedonistic Product.

Upon the selection of products that are bundled together, research shows that when bundling an expensive product together with a cheaper product, the value perception is reduced for the whole bundle [66]. This is because customers do not unilaterally add the values of the products together, but they "subtract" the price of the cheapest product. To subtract in this context means that the sum together is less than the prices individually. The subtracting effect occurs when a product comes from a product category with low-priced products. An experiment showed that when customers could choose between a one-year membership at a fitness center and equipment for home training, about half of the participants selected one option versus the other. When the home training was bundled with a free DVD, only 35 percent chose this option. The reason is that when adding a product to the low-price category, it reduces the perceived value of the bundle.

Add to small differences in prices for products that are similar. The idea of having endless choice options often leads to decision refusal. You do not want to miss out on the benefits of the other alternatives, and saying no to these feels like a loss. Humans have an inherent loss aversion. By creating *almost* equal choice options, the feeling of losses will be smaller [67], and it becomes easier to make a choice.

Research shows that few choices with small differences make it easier to make choices. In one study, two groups were given the choice between two different packets of chewing gum with the same price versus two packs with a small price difference [67].

Group 1: Two packs of chewing gum at the same price (example $1.40). Group 2: Two packs of chewing gum at a slightly different price (examples $1.40 and $1.50).

The interesting thing here is that even though the prices were almost identical, the price difference led more people to choose to buy chewing gum. The paradox is that at the same price, the participants found that the packages were different, and they were unable to choose. At different prices, they experienced the similarity as being greater, and this promoted a choice. This means that at the same price, customers must look for other prominent attributes of the products. When prices are different, it is easier to distinguish the products from each other.

Prepayment before consumption. When customers pay for a product or service *before* they receive it, they are aware of the benefits they will receive, which reduces the pain of having to pay. This effect has been tested in research, and the results show that prepayments are beneficial for all involved parties. The opposite is also true. If customers have already experienced the product, it feels considerably more painful to pay later [68]. This effect is useful for those who pay fixed terms, such as subscriptions. It will be most appropriate for customers to pay the subscription before they receive the magazine.

Partial payment is perceived as less painful. If you are about to split the price across several payments, the customer will consider the price as equivalent to the amount in the first payment. This results in cost being perceived as lower, and the threshold for buying increases. The comparison of numbers means that the smaller the parts you can divide the amount into, the lower the payment seems [69]. For products that are used every day, such as vitamins, the retailers often specify the price per day, in addition to the full price for the whole packet. Other examples of price division include the cost of each time you use the product, such as the cost per mile when driving an electric car.

A question many ask themselves is whether you should divide prices into a basic price and add secondary costs thereafter. Examples include shipping and delivery. A meta-analysis of the last 17 years of research on this [70] shows that most customers react more favorably to split prices because this makes them perceive the basic price as low. But this kind of price division also leads to less favorable preferences regarding the additional prices. An airline may therefore have prices with or without luggage, where the basic price is seen as low if it is without luggage prices, but customers will perceive the luggage costs as a major drawback.

Step 4: Use Discounts Correctly

Discounts are challenging because they can change the customers' reference price. They have taught customers that a product can be sold at lower prices. In the review of the various techniques below, I therefore discuss how you can use discounts in a better and smarter way.

Endowment effect is a theory that explains how we want to preserve the existing situation. This is the reason why we go for offers that promise us free installation or no fees for the first year, and why it hurts more to get rid of these products afterwards (therefore those who work in a clothing store should always try to get customers to try on the clothes, and car dealers should strive to get customers to test-drive cars).

In a well-known experiment, some researchers tested the endowment effect [71]. A group of students each received a coffee mug worth approximately $5. The students were then asked about the minimum price they were willing to sell the coffee mug for. A second group of students, who had not been offered any coffee mug, were asked how much money they were willing to receive as compensation for not receiving a coffee mug. Those who had received coffee mugs gave an average price of $7.12. Those who did not receive a coffee mug gave an average price of $3.12. This illustrates how the value of owning a coffee mug surpasses the price you are willing to pay for the same product.

Give a reason for the discount. For shops with EDLP (Every Day Low Prices), customers will react to discounted prices. The confidence in their price system programs is that they are always at the lowest limit. Discounts in such systems therefore require extra explanation so that customers perceive the price system as credible. This is done by providing customers with a reason: for example, that the new discounts come from suppliers and are passed on to the customers [72]. Such price communication can also help in specifying how long the price reduction is for: for example, that it applies to this one batch of goods. Such exceptions make customers understand that these are exceptional prices and not a permanent price change.

The less money we have in our account, the higher a price is perceived. This means a willingness to pay a higher price on the salary pay date than on the days before. This is a well-known strategy in the period when the tax money comes – the mailbox is flooded with offers for everything from new sofas to new beds. In fact, this tactic has research evidence. Research shows that the pain of payment is higher the less money you have available [73]. Paying $95 for a concert ticket is therefore perceived as far more expensive in the days before payday than in the days after. In other words, the more money you have in your account, the higher the willingness to pay. In the same way, discounts will be more important on days when you have less money in the account.

Discounts may harm the long-term sales. Discounts can be harmful because customers get an expectation of the next discount. Therefore, when you finish one rebate, this can lead to customers (a) choosing a competitor's product, or (b) waiting for the next discount.

The effects of a discount are strongest for products with high price sensitivity. For products where the price has little significance, discounts will have very little effect, and should be avoided. This is because the discounts on these products do not affect sales to a large extent [74], but in fact can lead to more damage because the customers are taught to focus on prices.

Price changes are perceived differently depending on whether the prices are set up or down. Studies on the implementation of discounts provide a clear recommendation on how these should be performed. The research recommends that you gradually return to the original price, instead of suddenly ending a campaign [75]. This means that the discount ranges, as an example, from 40 percent to 30 percent, 20 percent, and 10 percent, rather than going from 40 percent to 0 percent. The reason is that the declining discount acts as a signal effect to customers. If they wait, the price will return to the original price (see Figure 9.9).

If you are going to increase the price, do it in many small price increases. If you want to reduce the price, do it in few and large intervals. This logic is based on what is called the *Weber-Fechner law*, which is derived from physics [4]. Tiny

Discount change – leap-over		Discount change - gradual	
Period 1	40 %	Period 1	40 %
Period 2	40 %	Period 2	30 %
Period 3	0 %	Period 3	20 %
Period 4	0 %	Period 4	10 %
Period 5	0 %	Period 5	0 %

Figure 9.9: Leap-over versus Gradual Discount Change.

physical changes are not noticed, while large jumps are easy to detect. This is also the case with price changes.

Therefore, as prices change gradually upwards, customers will not notice the actual price increase to the same extent as if they took the price increases in larger jumps. A well-known example is petrol prices, which vary up and down around the clock, but which also have small price increases over time. At the same time, petrol prices are rising slowly but surely, without this feeling as dramatic. Therefore, do not wait too long to set the price. This also means that if you want to reduce prices, don't do this in small intervals as the customers will not notice the cost reduction to any great extent. Accordingly, the whole effect can be lost.

This also means that the sale of expensive products, for example an iPad at $200 that is reduced by 20 percent, should be communicated with the discounted in $, i.e., $40. For less expensive products, for example a book at $20, it is advisable to state the price reduction in percentage, i.e., 20 percent, rather than the amount of $4. Also, communicating rebates with precise numbers will be perceived as smaller. Therefore, rounded prices will be an advantage when communicating discounts [52].

Summary

This chapter shows that the perception of whether a price is high or low, acceptable, or unreasonable is affected by the way the figures are presented, the surrounding environment, customers' experiences, psychological processes, the risk around the purchases, and whether a purchase is a bargain with a deadline. In this chapter I have shown how the individual perception of a price, payment, or discount is affected by the number itself, but also by the visualization, the environment, and the way the price is combined with other prices. Proper handling of this can have positive effects on the business, while incorrect handling or utilization of customers is quite destructive. The chapter started with a description of the reference price and how customers focus on transaction benefits rather than the actual price they pay. A careful review of four steps that describe the use of psychological pricing has also been carried out.

Chapter 10
E-commerce and Prices in Digital Markets

Introduction

The boundaries between physical stores and the Internet are becoming less and less pertinent. Rather than seeing e-commerce as hard competitors to physical stores, we witness a development where they reinforce each other with the purpose of promoting sales experiences. We are in the middle of the development. Going a few years back in time, we were told the mantra that the "Internet leads to lower prices!" This was at the beginning of the e-commerce era. Firms expected a fierce price competition as well as the death of most of the physical stores. The argument was that information about prices on the Internet is freely available. It was assumed that the price increases would stimulate us all to make rational choices, i.e., choosing the products with the lowest prices. Research and analysis show a far more complex picture. In this chapter, I will go through the attributes of pricing in e-commerce. I have divided this into 10 steps and will discuss each in order. After this I discuss the development of the prices of e-commerce and digital markets, followed by a review of global actors in online sales. Finally, I discuss price robots and price comparison algorithms.

Steps in the Development of Prices in e-Commerce and Digital Markets

The premise that all information on the Internet is freely available is not true. The Internet has search friction [76]. This means that product options are not available for easy comparison. E-commerce consists of tens of thousands of products in huge varieties. The way a company presents, sorts, and groups lists of products influences customers' access to information and thereby their choice sets. Also, the structure of websites affects customer clicks [76], i.e., how many products a customer on average clicks on to get access to additional information. And not least, the number of clicks affects how many customers results in actual purchases. Fewer clicks lead to a higher probability of purchases [76].

E-commerce has undergone large development since the start. Customers now want something more than just a large product range. An example of innovation is real-time online shopping, where sales consultants in physical stores show the product selection to the customers via an online link. Other solutions include artificial intelligence (AI), where the customer can visualize the products in their reality, for example visualizing different colors on their wall, or how different furniture fits into their own living room. Customers also want faster delivery and haggle-free return on the goods they have ordered [77]. The largest network players are experimenting with

https://doi.org/10.1515/9783110987102-010

different solutions. This can be about cooperation with local distribution companies and guaranteed delivery of goods within an agreed time interval, cooperation with actors in the sharing economy where individuals take on the task of retrieving and delivering the goods, stations where customers can pick up prepackaged goods in the store or from physical cabinets/vending machines located in the neighborhood or along central arterial roads, supply delivered directly to the trunk of our car that is parked at our workplace, or unmanned drones that fly packages to your door within 30 minutes. The requirement for fast delivery puts new requirements on the logistics, and advanced algorithms help to estimate demand in specific geographical areas so that the inventory is continuously optimized.

The development of prices in e-commerce and digital markets has both similarities and differences with physical trade. Customer segmentation and value perception are largely based on the same factors. However, the way prices are presented, visualized, and framed is an especially important element in digital markets. This affects sales to a large degree. Research shows that online customer evaluations reduce customers' price sensitivity. This is because the information is perceived as reliable information about the true product quality. Online evaluations can thus be used as an indicator of future price changes as the evaluations reflect customers' price-benefit assessments [78].

Important elements to consider when pricing in e-commerce and digital markets are described in 10 steps below (see Figure 10.1).

Step 1: Visible Prices

Customers who must search, register email addresses, or take other actions to access prices have a greater tendency to drop out before the purchase is complete. In addition, skepticism about sharing private information has become much more prominent. Customers often do not want to leave e-mail addresses or telephone numbers. If competitors make prices easily accessible, it is likely that customers will choose this safe option rather than spend time searching for prices on your websites.

The digital world demands and expects quick responses. If you have a solution that requires registration of wishes and needs on a form, it can take many hours before the customer receives an answer. By that time the customer has most likely been lost a long time ago. Transparency about prices signals confidence in the market. The downside is, of course, that the competitors also see these prices. But a solid customer advantage and a healthy cost basis are often to be preferred. And customers who feel that they have paid too much are dissatisfied anyway.

In Chapter 9 about psychological pricing, I described how websites knowingly use psychological effects when they present prices to customers. This is therefore not repeated here. There is no doubt that the reference prices are affected by

Visibility	Bundling	Highlight	Visualization	Choices
Step 1:	Step 2:	Step 3:	Step 4:	Step 5:
Visible prices	Bundling price options	Highlight the best price option	Visual design of pricing options	Determine choice options

Deals	Value	Price models	Competitors	Additional services
Step 6:	Step 7:	Step 8:	Step 9:	Step 10:
Offers with subscriptions and time limits	The customer only buys value	Combine different pricing models	Map out competitors' prices	Pricing additional services

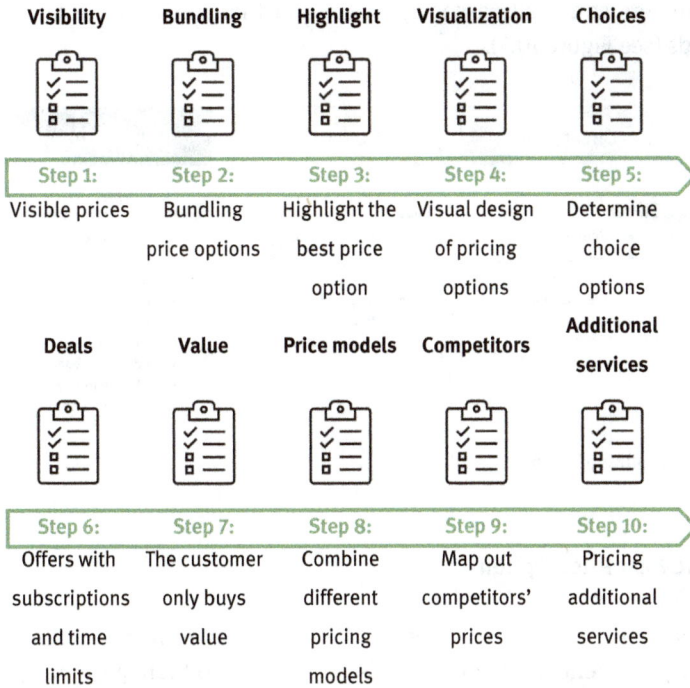

Figure 10.1: Steps in the Development of Prices in e-Commerce and Digital Markets.

numbers in the surroundings, including online. In online stores, this can be used knowing that you are exposing customers to other figures, including those that do not have a direct connection with the products sold (see Figure 10.2).

Pants $ 95
We also sell
Dresses for $195
Jackets for $155

Figure 10.2: Reference Prices for Online Shopping.

Step 2: Bundling Price Options

Bundling price alternatives follow the same structure as described for product bundling in Chapter 4 on different prices for the same products. The combination options are made available in clear tabular layout so that customers can easily compare the various package options. Remember that the variation between the bundles must be based on the different needs of the customer segments. Give each of the bundles a name that the customers can easily associate with, and that fits with the target group's various needs (see Figure 10.3).

Member Club	Silver Club	Gold Club	Black Club
Member: • Point collector • Save preferences • Member-only offers	**Silver:** • Point collector • Save preferences • Member-only offers • Free seating	**Gold:** • Point collector • Save preferences • Member-only offers • Free seating • Priority boarding • Lounge access	**Black:** • Point collector • Save preferences • Member-only offers • Free seating • Priority boarding • First lounge access • Additional baggage • 24/7 online support • Guarantee booking

Figure 10.3: Example of Bundling of Member Levels.

Step 3: Highlight the Best Price Option

It can be difficult for customers to take on board the various underlying details in product bundles. To help them along the way it is often smart to highlight one option as the best or most preferred. This is often done by using a different color and marking it as the "best option." Often the best alternative is placed in the middle. This helps customers make a choice in a situation with otherwise overwhelming information. The disadvantage of such a strategy is that those who would otherwise have chosen the most expensive option might now prefer the one in the middle.

In Chapter 9 on psychological pricing, we looked at the anchoring effect on prices. In online stores this can be used by marking how many others have chosen a particular option (example: 1,547 customers have chosen this option). This trigger anchoring effect results in a willingness to pay a higher price [79].

Step 4: Visual Design of Pricing Options

It is advantageous to present all the product packages on one screen page, so that customers do not have to scroll down to get complete information. Visual elements such as tabular layout, figures, and the use of color help customers in their decision-making (see Figure 10.4). Make sure that only the most important and necessary information for customers' decision-making is included. Everything else should come later so as not to overwhelm the customer with details.

Most popular	Best value	
Student edition	**Family edition**	**Business edition**
$ 49,99	$ 69,99	$ 149,99
★★★★☆	★★★★☆	
Applications included:	*Applications included:*	*Applications included:*
Text program	Text program	Text program
Spreadsheet program	Spreadsheet program	Spreadsheet program
Presentation program	Presentation program	Presentation program
	3 or more users	Company users
Service included:	*Service included:*	*Service included:*
Online customer support	Online customer support	(not included)
Sky storage	Sky storage	

Figure 10.4: Visual Design of Price Alternatives.

Step 5: Determine Choice Options and Price Combinations

Some products are more demanding and complex. In these cases, so-called "election calculators" are a good tool. A selection calculator includes the most important elements (often from 5 to 10 elements) that the buyer can select or opt out of (see Figure 10.5). By highlighting the options, they continuously get the final closing price, and the process becomes transparent. This helps the customer to evaluate only what they need or what

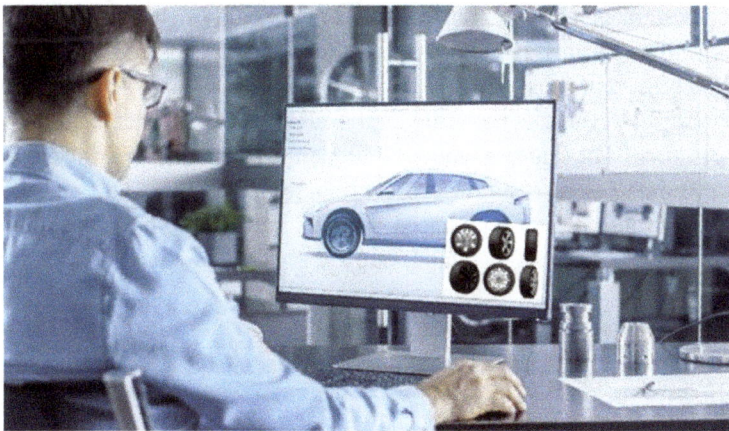

Figure 10.5: Choice Combinations in Price Calculator.

their economy can handle. The disadvantage is that customers see the partial prices and can use this information to switch to another supplier.

Step 6: Offers with Subscriptions and Time Limits

Digital online products are often sold with subscription schemes for specific time intervals. Customers can have options to choose from. For example, prices may be fixed for a specific period, for example one year, or vary according to time intervals, for example per month (see Figure 10.6). If customers' willingness to pay varies, is it most appropriate to give them various options. This ensures that most customers find an offer that is acceptable within their needs. However, it is important to calculate the income effect of giving a fixed price rather than a monthly price, so that the price combinations do not lead to an actual loss of income.

INTERNET SERVICE PROVIDER	ANNUAL EQUIPMENT RENTAL COSTS	MODEM/ROUTER PRICE
AP&S	$130	$235
CORTLEY	$190	$290
TELENIX	$145	$180
NOWFIX	$144	$185
XFIDELITY	$180	$265

Figure 10.6: Subscription Prices and Time Restrictions.

Step 7: The Customer only Buys Value

I return to this point repeatedly in the book. Customers only buy a product or service based on the value it provides to them, and not based on the company's costs. It can be difficult to map customers' perception of value and quantify it. But it is necessary if customers are to feel that they are gaining something from the purchase. At the beginning of the book I described practical steps to identify and quantify customer value (see Chapter 2). Remember, however, that the value for the customer can also include saved time and spared resources. For example, online IT support can lead to lower downtime for a business. Downtime can be quantified through losses in income. And finally, if you cannot deliver the value you have promised, you will not be long in the business. Do you have the capacity to deliver the online IT support system you promised?

Step 8: Combine Different Pricing Models

This point does not apply to everyone who sells in digital markets. But some, especially those who work in the business market, may have fewer customers who, due to their goals, have very specific needs. A company that wants to attach itself to an occupational health service may, for example, want to do this either at a fixed business price, or at a price per employee, or at a price based on the use of the service. This allows the customer to optimize the contract based on their specific needs. Again, it is important to create a price plan based on the actual customer needs and calculate the financial consequences.

Step 9: Map Out Competitors' Prices

Customers will most likely compare your prices with the prices of the closest competitors. This does not mean that they necessarily choose the cheapest alternative, but the competing prices will form a reference point against which they assess the prices. If your prices are far above or far below, they will be perceived as less credible. Competitors may also have other options and pricing models than the one you use. This provides important information for you to interpret the market. Remember, however, that your competitors may have a completely random pricing policy that is not based on a strategy or any specific tools. Pure copying can therefore lead to major damage.

Step 10: Pricing Additional Services

A critical question that many are struggling with is about whether to charge for additional services, such as technical support, or whether this should be included in the regular price. If the additional services have a great value for the customer, it could form the basis for a new source of income. It also gives the customer the opportunity to assess whether this is something they need and want to pay for. On the other hand, customers might suspect the product has weaknesses and that you want to exploit this through additional costs. Customers' perception about such matters is important to map out before you make a price division. Beside this, as mentioned previously, customers mostly prefer a low base price [23].

Online Sales and Global Players

Large online players such as *Amazon.com* vary their prices on average *10 times per hour* [80]. With the volume of products Amazon has in its portfolio, this amounts to 2.5 million changes every single day throughout the year. There is, of course, an extreme exploitation of all the 200 million customers they have in their big data portfolio that makes this possible. This is difficult to copy. Their volume outweighs the negative customer reactions, since the price variation increases sales by 25 percent. Few online stores can treat customers this way.

Big data provide advantages if they are used correctly. Large online players have enormous access to big data and an opportunity to utilize these to estimate customers' behavior. Analysis of big data has five attributes: volume – the large number of data points; *variation* – the data come from many different sources and in many different forms; *viscosity* – the data have enormous speed; *validity* – the data are often incomplete; and *value* – the data can be linked to purchasing behavior and value estimates [81]. Under the precondition that the data are analyzed based on customers' capabilities and limitations, they provide an opportunity to estimate consumer behavior in detail. An example of such analysis is product recommendations based on previous web searches. This can lead to additional sales. Analyzing big data is sometimes unnecessary, while in other cases it requires specialist expertise [81]. The ability to utilize data in analysis with the purpose of predicting behavior is considered an important investment.

Aliexpress.com is a giant Chinese online player targeting the consumer goods market. A second player, *Alibaba.com*, aims toward the business market. Both players offer products at very low prices. However, it is important to be aware of replicas, i.e., counterfeit and illegal products, of all global online players.

Most well-known global brand companies, such as Gant, combine many different online players to be present in the online market. This is everything from your own online store to major players such as *Zalando.com* and *Boozt.com*.

The long tail is an expression that describes the strategy of new international online businesses that rely on selling very small volumes to many different customers based on a wide range of products over time. The term is based on the 80/20 rule, which means that 80 percent of the income comes from 20 percent of the product range. The Internet enables this type of online sales on a global basis. Online solutions such as *Ebay.com* make it easier for independent retailers to offer their products to many customers. An example of an online store for small private producers is *Etsy.com*. Recent research shows that customers are less price sensitive when they associate the provider with a local affiliation [26]. Global players who manage to trigger a local identity for their brands will therefore experience a lower price sensitivity.

Price Robots and Price Comparisons

A price robot is an algorithm (computer program) that scans websites for prices of different products from different players. There are many free computer programs that enable such web scraping, including Google extensions. Setting up such web scraping is not particularly difficult, and several YouTube videos show you how to do it step by step. Of course, there are companies that can do it for you. Anyway, the online companies are often not interested in this type of data collection, and several now put constraints on their web pages to make it more difficult to automatically capture their prices. Price robots are most effective in industries where there are dynamic prices, such as hotels and air tickets. However, we see that hourly price variations are also increasing in new industries, such as electronics.

PriceGrabber and *PriceRunner* are two of the many actors who are working on comparing prices on online products. Customers can click on their web pages and see price comparisons in various categories and products and click on links to get direct access to the service provider. A problem with the neutrality of such price spies is that many of them deliberately highlight players they have entered into cooperation with. However, the price comparison companies are often completely open about these types of priorities, provided you read the small text at the bottom of the web page.

There are also other price comparison players. Also, some of the actors base their price comparisons on specific selected brands, which makes comparison across brands difficult. In addition, the prices stated on international websites are often not comparable with the final price paid by the customer. Examples include the addition of customs, VAT, shipping, and taxes. Note that the EU imposes the inclusion of the full price when shopping online.

Summary

This chapter shows that pricing for online sales and digital products largely follows the same logic as pricing in physical trade, even though online solutions enable more pricing tools, such as price calculators. Online sales also have peak load pricing, which means that the willingness to pay for a product is higher during special holidays, such as at Christmas. Changing prices is easy when they are digital. But it comes with an important warning. A price that is lowered for a short period of time can be very difficult to raise. This is because customers have learned that you can sell the products cheaper than you normally do. Other industries are well known for varying prices continuously.

Chapter 11
Prices in the Sharing Economy

Introduction

Everyone knows Airbnb and Uber in the sharing economy. But did you know that you can also get help to buy organic vegetables or borrow another family's dog? In this chapter, I will go through five steps to work with price in the sharing economy. This is about determining the customers, knowing the competitors, mapping the attributes of the products/services, quantifying customer value, and calculating the total economic value to the customers.

Sharing Economy and Sharing Platforms

The sharing economy differs from other types of transactions in that (1) it uses digital platforms that facilitate transaction activity, (2) the ownership rights to the product or the services are not transferred (except through the sale of used private products), and (3) the activity mainly consists of sharing between private persons [82]. The main idea is that available resources in households are made available to others. Figure 11.1 shows an excerpt of the possibilities within the sharing economy.

There are several advantages to the sharing economy as seen from a customer perspective. Because it is based on available resources, the provider has no capital-intensive investment as a basis. These reduced costs can be utilized through competitive lower prices. In addition, since customers must not invest in capital-intensive goods either, this gives them greater flexibility in terms of choice and consumption. And not least, many customers emphasize the sustainability aspect of sharing; it increases capacity utilization and reduces waste. Studies show that customers respond positively to such measures, and that brands are not harmed by this type of price reduction [42]. As an example, an analysis shows that a private car is parked as much as 95 percent of the time, and the popularity of car-sharing services is growing rapidly [82]. To analyze the pricing strategy of the sharing economy, the first step it to identify and map how it creates customer value, and what competitive advantage it provides. Figure 11.2 provides a good overview of the classification of the sharing economy. The figure has three axes. It distinguishes between the degree of manual versus cognitive activities, labor-intensive versus capital-intensive services, and routine tasks versus nonroutine tasks.

https://doi.org/10.1515/9783110987102-011

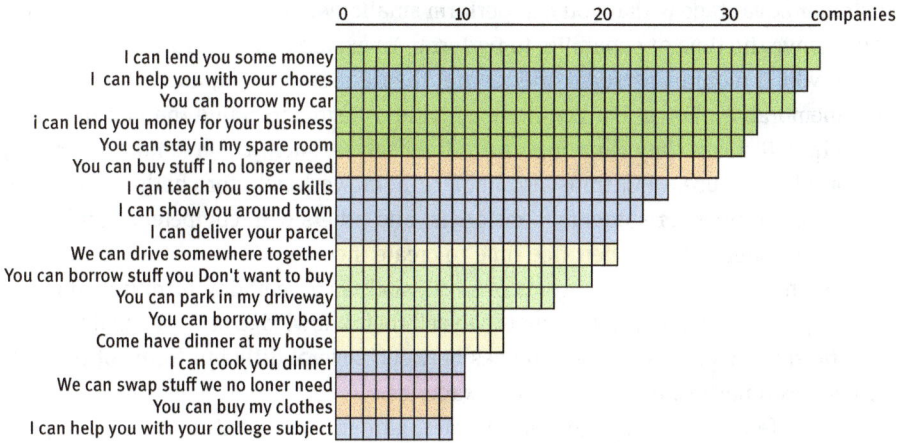

Figure 11.1: List of Various Services within the Sharing Economy. Retrieved from https://www.just park.com/creative/sharing-economy-index/. The website has a list of more than 250 services and over 800 players (as of January 2022).

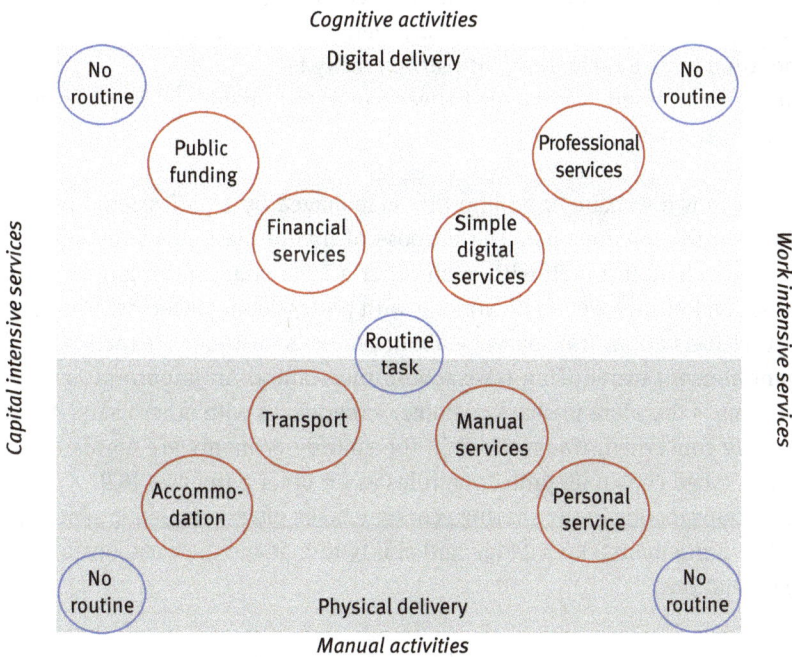

Figure 11.2: Services Provided through Digital Platforms (Sharing Economy) [82].

For capital-intensive services, the customer advantage lies in the fact that customers do not have to tie up capital. By choosing services through the sharing economy, customers get more room for maneuver. For labor-intensive services, the customer advantage is that you can perform smaller work tasks that you do not otherwise have the time or capability to perform. An example of this is wedding photography, which requires personal attendance, the right equipment, and competence to take memorable photos. For cognitive activities, customers value the fact that they get help with tasks they cannot perform themselves, such as personal accounting, learning how to use a PC, translator help, or homework help for children. This provides opportunities for students, pensioners, and others with competence and spare capacity to offer some of their free time to create income. When it comes to manual activity one can offer various forms of work, such as assembling furniture, shelves, cleaning, and gardening. Hobby chefs can sell their knowledge or ready-made food.

The sharing economy distinguishes between several different forms of transaction between parties. Here are several examples:

- Rental (e.g., home, cottage, car, bicycles, garden equipment, tools, etc.) https://turo.com/
- Loans (e.g., garden furniture for a party in the neighborhood) https://www.peerby.com
- Access and service (e.g., courses and training) https://www.khanacademy.org/
- Sharing (e.g., Internet, transport) https://fon.com/
- Donations (e.g., surplus products) https://energizelives.gridmates.com/
- Collaboration (e.g., food sharing) https://sharecity.ie/
- Exchanges (e.g., home exchanges between private individuals) https://www.lovehomeswap.com/

A *digital platform* is a website or an app that is managed by a professional player, like the URLs on the previous list. The purpose of digital platforms is twofold: to put buyers and sellers in touch with each other and to share information about price and quality. Because we're not working with professional players who are regulated by strict legislation, transparency about previous customers' experiences is an important element in reducing transaction uncertainty. An important task for digital platforms is therefore to share customer experiences with other users. As far as legislation is concerned, transactions in the sharing economy are regulated by the same established consumer protection rules as for other purchases [82].

Note that transactions in the sharing economy takes place between individuals. This can affect participants' knowledge and ability to manage their responsibilities within the regulations.

Differences between Sharing Economy and Traditional Economy

An important factor in the sharing economy is the role of customers in what is called "prosumption." "Prosumption" is a term formed from the words "production" and "consumption." In other words, customers participate in creating their own consumption. Examples of "presumption" include the development of Wikipedia, where users write, edit, update, and comment on articles. YouTube, Flickr, Pinterest, and blogs are all created by users who upload videos, pictures, and texts. Virtual game worlds consist of players who create characters, societies, and worlds. Facebook, Twitter, and LinkedIn are created by people who create profiles and share content with others. One of the biggest challenges in "presumption" is therefore the quality variations and the quality uncertainty it can entail [83].

The consequence of "presumption" in the sharing economy is that instuitions, i.e., businesses or enterprises, are replaced by customers. This challenges the existing legislation, which must intend to protect the customer. As an example: For the car sharing solutions Uber and Lyft, a "prosumer" both consumes the car and offers services (such as coordinating, collecting, running, bringing) to those who are riding. The driver gives an assessment of the customer, and the customer gives an assessment of the driver. In the traditional economy, a customer assesses satisfaction with the use of a product. In the sharing economy, even the users themselves are evaluated.

In the traditional economy, dynamic competitive advantages create the basis for value creation. In the sharing economy, we often see that one winner takes large parts of the market. Thus, the first-to-market advantages are often of far greater importance in these markets [83]. The competition in the sharing economy can in many cases be harder because the providers compete both internally with each other (cf. Uber and Lyft) and also with the traditional companies (taxis).

One of the hallmarks of the sharing economy is the way it creates temporary access to a product or service. This also affects the pricing strategy, which is often far more dynamic based on offer and demand in the market. Top load prices are more common.

Steps to Set Prices in the Sharing Economy

It can be difficult to decide on the prices for services (and products) in the sharing economy. How much is the spare capacity for you or your equipment worth? What one must do is to practically calculate how much benefit a customer will have from the service. Remember that a customer does not buy anything based on your available capacity or what costs you have. They are only concerned with their own value and utility they get from spending their money. The procedure for quantifying the price follows the same steps as described elsewhere in the book (see Figure 11.3). Simplified, this is as follows:

Customers	Competitors	Attributes	Customer value	Economic value
Step 1:	Step 2:	Step 3:	Step 4:	Step 5:
Determine customer segments	Map competing players	Map differentiation attributes	Quantify customer value	Calculate total economic value

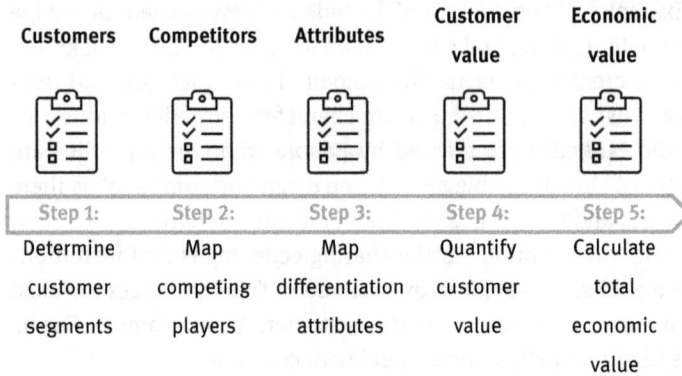

Figure 11.3: Steps in VTC Analysis in the Sharing Economy.

Step 1: Determine Customer Group

Decide which customer segment you have the greatest chance of succeeding with. A common mistake that entrepreneurs and startup companies make is to assume that their product or service is so amazing that everyone will want to buy it. This may be the case, but at the same time there are some customer segments that are easier to convince and succeed with than others. These customers are the best (and easiest) to start with, and then you can take the whole world domination thing step by step later.

Step 2: Map Competing Players

Identify the price of competing services that customers can choose (both from professional firms and from the actors in the sharing economy). This means simply asking what customers would have chosen if your service did not exist.

Step 3: Mapping Differentiation Attributes

Map which attributes of your service are *different* from attributes of competing services. This means both where you are better and where you are worse.

Step 4: Determine Customer Value

Map what value *customers* attach to these attributes. NB: only the attributes that are different! Use the Excel analysis to identify the *value of attributes* as explained and illustrated in Chapter 3 in this book.

Step 5: Calculate Total Economic Value

Add the numbers and estimate the total economic value for the customers. Use this as a starting point for the *maximum price* you can charge in the market. A common mistake one makes in this process is to forget that the attributes in Step 3 must be *visible, clear, and important* for the customers when they make their purchase decisions.

Disadvantages with the Sharing Economy

One of the disadvantages you have within the price strategy in the sharing economy is that you do not get any help from the other product categories. A grocery store may have a low price on turkey to attract customers to the store. They cover the loss through additional sales that the customer attraction entails. In the sharing economy, one seldom has such a product portfolio to lean on. In addition, the sharing platform makes it difficult to build loyal customers, which means that each transaction is often traded individually. The sharing economy also makes it more difficult to facilitate additional sales. For example, an Airbnb room will not be able to sell a tour guide as an extra service. A second effect that applies to services and pricing is that when customers are exposed to prices during their experience, this leads to reduced satisfaction. The reason is that customers' attention is drawn to the financial aspect of the transaction in place rather than the experience [84].

Circular Economy and Price

In the circular economy, the sharing platforms Tise.com and Ebay.com are widely used for buying and selling used clothes and interior items. The research of López-Fernández [85] shows that the millennial generation is less price sensitive to product attributes in that they prefer ethical consumption over low price when factors such as social responsibility are considered.

Another example is the "Too Good To Go" app, where unsold food and leftovers are sold at greatly reduced prices in several major cities in the US and Europe. The purpose is to stop food waste.

The waste hierarchy is often illustrated through an inverted triangle (see Figure 11.4). The lowest level is landfilling (putting in landfill), followed by energy utilization (burning), material recycling (making new from used), reuse (using things again), and waste reduction (producing less waste). Producing less waste means in practice that one should avoid shopping. Reuses are the purchase and sale of used clothing, interior items, electronics, sports equipment, and so on. Equipment repair is included in this section.

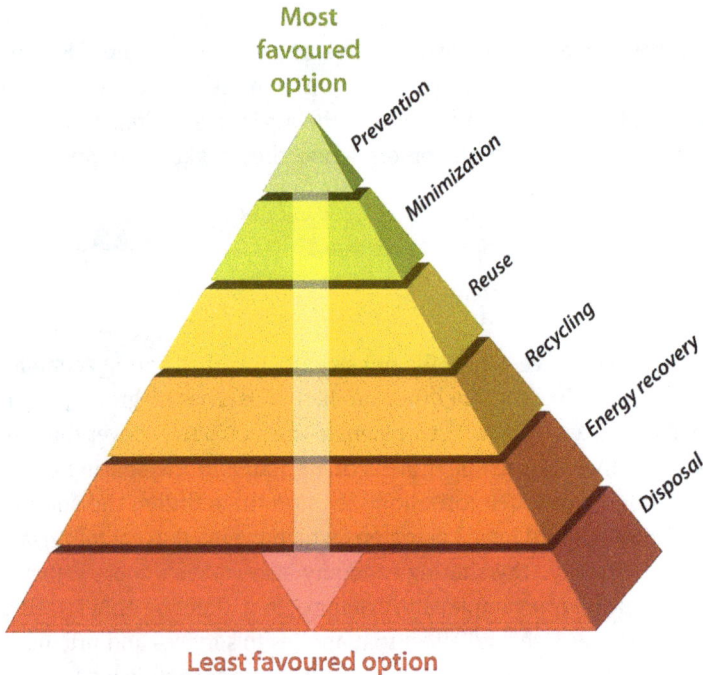

Figure 11.4: The Waste Hierarchy.

Marketing tools can be used to change consumer behavior towards more sustainable consumption [86] by moving them upwards in the triangle. The role of price in such a system is described by White et al. [86]. They point out that incentives in the form of rewards, refunds, gifts, and other external incentives can promote desirable behavior and create positive habits. Incentives have been shown to promote sustainable behavior in terms of waste management and cleanup, energy use, and the choice of transport. However, they point out that short-term incentives lead to short-term changes. Even if customers immediately react positively to the incentives, this disappears equally fast when the incentives are gone. In addition, it can harm the intrinsic motivation of involvement. The millennial generation's focus on, and motivation for, sustainability can therefore be damaged by incorrect use of price as an incentive tool.

By this I mean that an excessive emphasis on price campaigns to stimulate sustainability can have a destructive effect on the intrinsic motivation.

Summary

The sharing economy is increasing in scope, not least due to the increased attention to consumption, resource use, reuse, and multiple use. In this chapter, I have shown how price is specifically used in the sharing economy. The chapter explains the difference between the sharing economy and the traditional economy. Then I highlight five steps that will help the reader maneuver prices in these sharing markets. Finally, there is a section on price in the circular economy.

Chapter 12
Pricing Calculations

Introduction

I then go through various pricing strategies at the end and round off with profitability analysis and price elasticity analysis.

Significance of Costs

Two companies that have completely different cost structures will experience very *similar* prices for the products in the market [3]. This is a clear signal that companies' costs are of little importance when customers are making a purchase. One of the most common mistakes made when you determine a pricing strategy is to start with your internal costs. As mentioned under value-based pricing, one should rather start with the value added of the product or service given to the customers, and on this basis define the costs that can be justified, i.e., for materials, processes, production, and distribution. Another mistake made, especially for new development and innovation, is to calculate too short a timespan for covering innovation costs. Often a company seeks to cover its costs as quickly as possible. In addition, incorrect costs are included in the calculation.

The costs do not affect the price but are important for calculating whether different production and sales intervals are profitable or not. To identify costs that have an impact on profitability, it is common to distinguish between two types of costs, namely variable costs and fixed costs.

Variable costs are incurred only when the units are manufactured or sold. These are costs that can be traced directly back to a particular product. In complex companies, it can be difficult to separate the costs of the actual production or sales. Examples of variable costs include hourly wages for production employees, sales bonuses, raw materials, development costs, packaging, advertising, electricity for production, and company cars for the salespeople.

Fixed costs do not vary with production. All costs that cannot be attributed to a particular product or sales are considered fixed costs. Examples include salaries for the administration, interest and payment on loans, rent, deduction on machines and equipment, electricity for office buildings, and insurance.

In periods when the company is working to establish themselves, they must accept not being able to cover all regular costs. After a time, these costs must also be covered for the company to be able to continue their production and sales. Fewer units sold will transfer a large proportion of the fixed costs of these products, which

https://doi.org/10.1515/9783110987102-012

leads to a need for higher prices. Costs are affected by volume, and volume is affected by price. In the long run, of course, all costs must be covered. No business can survive with long-term losses. At the same time, it is important to be aware of the costs that can be identified in the market.

Factors that identify the cost picture:
1. What are the costs of existing and new competitors?
2. What are the costs of commercializing the products?
3. What costs do customers have?

Competitor costs, both existing and new, provide insights into their competitiveness, financial strength, and endurance ability. It also signals their expansion and innovation opportunities.

Commercialization costs are direct costs related to research and development, production, and commercialization, including sales, promotion, launch, and all future costs that are directly related to the product.

Customers' costs are identified through an economic value analysis, as described at the beginning of the book.

Calculation of Profitability Analysis

Calculation of profitability analysis is important for understanding the consequences of price changes for sales and number of units sold. The most common profitability calculations are given with example calculations in Tables 12.1 and 12.2.

Table 12.1: Profitability Calculations with TV as an Example.

Analysis	Formulas	Sales of TV
	P = Price	$P = 2500$
	V = Volume	$V = 1400$
	S = Sales	$S = 2500 \times 1400 = 3\,500\,000$
	VC = Variable Costs	$VC = 850$
	FC = Fixed Costs	$FC = 1\,200\,000$
1. Calculate Contribution Margin (CM)		
Contribution Margin (CM) means how much each unit sold contributes to covering fixed costs (FC) and profits	$CM = P - VC$	$CM = 2500 - 850 = 1650$ <u>Each TV has \$1 650 in contribution margin to cover fixed costs and profits</u>

Table 12.1 (continued)

Analysis	Formulas	Sales of TV
2. Calculate Profit Margin (PM)		
Profit Marin (PM) is profit as a % of sales turnover. It tells about the company's vulnerability compared to industry standard	$PM = \dfrac{(\text{Profit} \times 100)}{\text{Sales}}$	Profit = Sales − Total CM − FC Total CM = $1650 \times 1400 = 2\,310\,000$ Profit = $2310 - 1200 = 111\,0000$ $PM = \dfrac{(1\,110\,000 \times 100)}{3\,500\,000} = 31.7$ <u>Profit margin are 31,7%</u>
3. Calculate PM with price changes		
Price increases with 10%	$CM = (P + \Delta P) - VC$	$CM = (2\,500 + 10\%) - 850 = 1900$ <u>Contribution margin are $1\,900 at a price increase of 10%</u>
Price reduces with 10%	$CM = (P - \Delta P) - VC$	$CM = (2\,500 - 10\%) - 850 = 1400$ <u>Contribution margin are $1\,400 at a price reduction of 10%</u>
4. Calculate sales change with price changes		
How much can the sales be reduced to have at least the same profit at a price increase of 10%	$\Delta V = V - \dfrac{(\text{Profit} \times FC)}{\text{CM at price increase}}$	$\Delta V = 1400 - \dfrac{(1110' \times 1\,200')}{1900} = 184,2$ <u>They can sell 185 fewer units to obtain the same profit with a price increase of 10%</u>
Calculate how much the sales must increase to have at least the same profit at a price reduction of 10%	$\Delta V = V - \dfrac{(\text{Profit} \times FC)}{\text{CM at price decrease}}$	$\Delta V = 1400 - \dfrac{(1110' + 1\,200')}{1400} = 250$ <u>They must sell 250 units more to obtain the same profit with a price decrease of 10%</u>
5. Calculate Contribution Margin Ratio (CMR)		
Contribution Margin Ratio (CMR) is the percentage of the price that is left to cover fixed costs and profits	$CMR = \dfrac{(CM \times 100)}{P}$	$CMR = \dfrac{(1650 \times 100)}{2\,500} = 66$ <u>The Contribution Margin Ratio is 66% at a sales price of $2\,5000</u>
6. Calculate Contribution Margin Ratio (CMR) at price changes		
CMR at a +10% Price-increase	$CMR = \dfrac{(CM\ \text{new Price} \times 100)}{\text{new Price}}$	$CMR = \dfrac{(1900 \times 100)}{2\,750} = 69$ <u>The Contribution Margin Ratio is 69% at a sales price of $2\,750</u>

Table 12.1 (continued)

Analysis	Formulas	Sales of TV
CMR at a–10% Price-reduction	$CMR = \dfrac{(CM\ new\ Price \times 100)}{new\ Price}$	$CMR = \dfrac{(1400 \times 100)}{2\,250} = 62$ The Contribution Margin Ratio is 62% at a sales price of $2 250
7. Calculate Break Even Point (BEP)		
Break Even point (BEP) identifies how much you need in sales to cover all costs, both variable and fixed.	$BEP\ in\ \$ = \dfrac{FC}{CMR}$	$BEP\ in\ \$ = \dfrac{1\,200\,000}{0.66} = 1818181$ Break Even Point is $1 818 181

The most common expressions are the following:

– *Contribution margin* (CM) – how much each unit sold contributes to covering fixed costs (FC) and profits.
– *Profit margin* (PM) – profit as a percentage of sales turnover. Tells something about the company's vulnerability and is compared with industry standards.
– *Sales change in the event of a price change* – how many unit sales can be changed to achieve at least the same profit as before the price change.
– *Contribution margin ratio* (CMR) – the percentage of the price that is left to cover fixed costs and profits.
– *Breakeven point* (BEP) – how much you must have, either in turnover or selling units, to cover all costs, both variable and fixed.

These calculations often simplify the situation by taking one product as the basis for the analysis. This is rarely the case in the real world. For calculations of the breakeven point in $ one often uses the average number based on the whole range of products. Breakeven point sales in units are therefore impossible to calculate for more complicated product ranges.

– Each TV has $1,650 as a contribution margin to cover fixed costs and profit.
– They can sell 185 fewer units to achieve the same profit when the price is increased by 10 percent.
– They must sell 250 units more to achieve the same profit when the price is reduced by 10 percent.
– Each coffee mug has $3 as a contribution margin to cover fixed costs and profit.
– They can sell 107,142 units less to achieve the same profit with a price increase of 10 percent.
– They must sell 150,000 more units to achieve the same profit with a price reduction of 10 percent.

Table 12.2: Profitability Calculations with Coffee Mug as an Example.

Analysis	Formulas	Sales of coffee mugs
	P = Price V = Volume S = Sales VC = Variable Costs FC = Fixed Costs	P = 5 V = 750 000 S = 5 × 750 000 = 3 750 000 VC = 2 FC = 2 000 000

1. Calculate Contribution Margin (CM)

Contribution Margin (CM) means how much each unit sold contributes to covering fixed costs (FC) and profits	CM = P − VC	CM = 5 − 2 = 3 Each coffee mug has $3 in contribution margin to cover fixed costs and profits

2. Calculate Profit Margin (PM)

Profit Marin (PM) is profit as a % of sales turnover. It tells about the company's vulnerability compared to industry standard	$PM = \dfrac{\text{Profit} \times 100}{\text{Sales}}$	Profit = Sales − Total CM − FC Total CM = 3 × 750' = 2 250' Profit = 2 250' − 2 000' = 250 000 $PM = \dfrac{2500\ 000 \times 100}{3\ 750\ 000} = 6.66$ Profit margin are 6,67%

3. Calculate PM with price changes

Price increases with 10%	CM = (P + ΔP) − VC	CM = (5 + 10%) − 2 = 3.5 Contribution margin are $ 3.50 at a price increase of 10%
Price reduces with 10%	CM = (P − ΔP) − VC	CM = (5 − 10%) − 2 = 2.5 Contribution margin are $ 2.50 at a price reduction of 10%

4. Calculate sales change with price changes

How much can the sales be reduced to have at least the same profit at a price increase of 10%	$\Delta V = V - \dfrac{(\text{Profit} \times \text{FC})}{\text{CM at price increase}}$	$\Delta V = 750\ 000 - \dfrac{250 \times 2\ 000}{3,5} = 107\ 142$ They can sell 107 142 fewer units to obtain the same profit with a price increase of 10%
Calculate how much the sales must increase to have at least the same profit at a price reduction of 10%	$\Delta V = V - \dfrac{(\text{Profit} + \text{FC})}{\text{CM at price decrease}}$	$\Delta V = 750\ 000 - \dfrac{250' + 2\ 000'}{2,5} = 150$ They must sell 150 000 units more to obtain the same profit with a price decrease of 10%

Table 12.2 (continued)

Analysis	Formulas	Sales of coffee mugs
5. Calculate Contribution Margin Ratio (CMR)		
Contribution Margin Ratio (CMR) is the percentage of the price that is left to cover fixed costs and profits	$CMR = \dfrac{CM \times 100}{P}$	$CMR = \dfrac{3 \times 100}{5} = 60$ The Contribution Margin Ratio is 60% at a sales price of $5
6. Calculate Contribution Margin Ratio (CMR) at price changes		
CMR at a +10% Price-increase	$CMR = \dfrac{(CM\,new\,Price \times 100)}{new\,Price}$	$CMR = \dfrac{3,5 \times 100}{5,5} = 63,6$ The Contribution Margin Ratio is 63,6% at a sales price of $5,5
CMR at a−10% Price-reduction	$CMR = \dfrac{(CM\,new\,Price \times 100)}{new\,Price}$	$CMR = \dfrac{2,5 \times 100}{4,5} = 55,5$ The Contribution Margin Ratio is 55,5% at a sales price of $4,5
7. Calculate Break Even Point (BEP)		
Break Even Point (BEP) identifies how much you need in sales to cover all costs, both variable and fixed.	$BEP\ in\ \$ = \dfrac{FC}{CMR}$	$BEP\ in\ \$ = \dfrac{2\,000\,000}{0.60} = 333333$ Break Even Point is $333 333

Calculation of Price Elasticity and Cross-Price Elasticity

Previously in the book, I defined price *elasticity* as the percentage change in demand divided by the percentage change in price. Price elasticity is most often negative: It will say that you buy less of a product if the price increases.

For substitute products, such as Pepsi Max and Coca-Cola without sugar, a price change for one product directly affects the sales of other products. Substitute products are often found within the product categories. In Table 12.3 I show calculations of cross-price elasticity for *substitute products* and in Table 12.4 cross-price elasticity for *complementary products*.

- The average customer buys two bags of flower soil per rose bush.
- The average customer buys a bottle of rose fertilizer per rose bush.
- Sales can be reduced by 15 percent if the price is increased by 5 percent when there are no substitute products with cross-price elasticity.

Table 12.3: Cross-Price Elasticity of Substitute Products.

Analysis of substitute products	Sales of chocolate cereal	Sales of Muesli cereal
P Price per unit	P = 3.59	P = 3.05
VC Variable costs	VC = 2.54	VC = 1.35
CM Contribution Margin	CM = 3.59 − 2.54 = 1.05	CM = 3.05 − 1.35 = 1.70
CMR Contribution Margin Ratio		

1. Calculate Contribution Margin Ratio (CMR) with a price increase of +5% and no cross-price elasticity (CPE)

CMR without cross-price elasticity	$CMR = \dfrac{CM}{P} = \dfrac{1.05}{3.59} = 0.29 = 29\%$
	The Contribution Margin Ratio with a price increase of 5% is 29% when there is no cross-price elasticity

2. Calculate Break Even Point (BEP) in % of sales and no cross-price elasticity (CPE)

BEP without cross-price elasticity	$\Delta BEP = \dfrac{\Delta P}{(CMR + \Delta P)} = \dfrac{-0.5}{(29+5)} = -0.147$
	The sales can be reduced with 15% if the price increases with 5% and there is no substitute cross-price elasticity. If the sales are reduced with more than 15% the company will loose on the price increase.

3. Calculate Break Even Point (BEP) in % of sales when the price increases with 5% and half of the customers switch product (CPE)

CPE = Cross Price Elasticity	$\Delta CM = CM - (CPE \times CM substitute) = 1.05 - (0.5 \times 1.70) = 2.00$
	$\Delta CMR = \dfrac{CM substitute}{P} = \dfrac{1.70}{3.59} = 0.47$
	$\Delta BEP = \dfrac{-\Delta P}{(\Delta CMR + \Delta P)} = \dfrac{-0.5}{(47+0.5)} = -10$
	The sales can be reduced with 10% with a 5 % price increase and there are 50% cross price elasticity with substitute products. If the sales are reduced with more than 10% the company will loose on the price increase

- If the sales reduction is larger than 15 percent, the company will lose on the price increase.
- Sales can be reduced by 10 percent if the price is increased by 5 percent when there are substitute products with cross-price elasticity.
- If the sales reduction is greater than 10 percent, the company will lose on the price increase.
- Sales must be increased by 25 percent if the price is reduced by 10 percent when there are no complementary products with cross-price elasticity.
- If the sales increase is under 25 percent, the company will lose on the price reduction.

Table 12.4: Cross-Price Elasticity of Complementary Products.

Analysis of complementary products			
	Rose bushes	Flower soil	Rose fertilizers
P Price per unit	P = 49.9	P = 19.9	P = 15.0
VC Variable costs	VC = 25.0	VC = 5.0	VC = 9.0
CM Contribution Margin	CM = 24.9	CM = 14.9	CM = 6.0
CMR Contribution Margin Ratio			

1. Calculate Break Even Point (BEP) with a price reduction of –10% and no cross-price elasticity (CPR)

BEP without cross-price elasticity	$CMR = \dfrac{CM}{P} = \dfrac{24.9}{49.9} = 0.498$
	$\Delta BEP = \dfrac{\Delta P}{CMR + \Delta P} = \dfrac{-(-10)}{(50 + (-10))} = 0.25$
	The sales must increase with 25% if the price reduces with 10% and there is no cross-price elasticity of complementary products. If the sales are increased with less than 25% the company will loose on the price reduction.

2. Calculate Break Even Point (BEP) with a price reduction of –10% and cross-price elasticity (CPR)

	Rose bush	Flower soil	Rose fertilizers
CPE Cross Price Elasticity		An average customer buys two bags of flower foil per rose bush	An average customer buys ½ bottle of rose fertilizer per rose bush
ΔCM Contribution Margin	$\Delta CM = CM + (CPE \times CM\text{complementary})$ $\Delta CM = 24.9 + (2 \times 14.9) + (0.5 \times 6.0) = 57.7$		
ΔCMR Contribution Margin Ratio	$\Delta CMR = \dfrac{CM\text{complementary}}{P} = \dfrac{57.7}{49.9} = 1.15 = 115\%$		
ΔBEP Break Even Point	$\Delta BEP = \dfrac{-\Delta P}{(\Delta CMR + \Delta P)} = \dfrac{-10}{(115 + 10)} = .095$ The sales must increase with 10% with a 10% price increase and there is cross price elasticity among complementary products. If the sales are increased with less than 10% the company will loose on the price reduction		

- Sales must increase by about 10 percent if the price is reduced by 10 percent when there are complementary products with cross-price elasticity.
- If sales increase by less than 10 percent, the company will lose on the price reduction.

Summary

This chapter ended the book with a review of the company's costs and their significance, and then looked at various profitability analyses, and price elasticity analyses. All analysis is illustrated using clear numerical examples.

References

[1]   Liozu, S. and A. Hinterhuber, *Pricing as a driver of profitable growth: An agenda for CEOs and senior executives*. Business Horizons, 2021.

[2]   Mattos, A.L., J.C.T. Oyadomari, and F.N. Zatta, *Pricing Research: State of the Art and Future Opportunities*. SAGE Open, 2021. **11**(3): p. 21582440211032168.

[3]   Hoch, S. and V. Rao, *Review on Impact of Pricing Policy in an Organization*. IAA Journal of Scientific Research, 2020. **6**(1): p. 13–19.

[4]   Nagle, T.T. and G. Muüller, *The strategy and tactics of pricing: a guide to growing more profitably*. 2018, Routledge: New York, New York;,London, England.

[5]   Busse, M.R., A. Israeli, and F. Zettelmeyer, *Repairing the damage: the effect of price knowledge and gender on auto repair price quotes*. Journal of Marketing Research, 2017. **54**(1): p. 75–95.

[6]   Monroe, K., *Pricing: Making Profitable Decisions, 3rd Int. ed*. New York: MacGraw-Hill, 2005.

[7]   Liozu, S.M. and A. Hinterhuber, *Pricing orientation, pricing capabilities, and firm performance*. Management Decision, 2013. **51**(3): p. 594–614.

[8]   Hinterhuber, A. and S.M. Liozu, *Is innovation in pricing your next source of competitive advantage?*, in *Innovation in Pricing*. 2017, Routledge. p. 11–27.

[9]   Hinterhuber, A., T.C. Snelgrove, and B.-I. Stensson, *Value first, then price: the new paradigm of B2B buying and selling*. Journal of Revenue and Pricing Management, 2021. **20**(4): p. 403–409.

[10] Liozu, S.M., *State of value-based-pricing survey: Perceptions, challenges, and impact*. Journal of Revenue and Pricing Management, 2017. **16**(1): p. 18–29.

[11] Zeithaml, V.A., *Consumer perceptions of price, quality, and value: a means-end model and synthesis of evidence*. Journal of Marketing, 1988. **52**(3): p. 2–22.

[12] Murphy, P.E. and B.M. Enis, *Classifying products strategically*. Journal of Marketing, 1986. **50**(3): p. 24–42.

[13] Jacoby, J. and L.B. Kaplan. *The components of perceived risk*. in *SV – Proceedings of the Third Annual Conference of the Association for Consumer Research*. 1972. Chicago.

[14] Dholakia, U.M., *A quick guide to value-based pricing*, in *Harvard Business Review*. 2016.

[15] Singh, J., *Value-based pricing: Two easy steps to implement and two common pitalls to avoid.*, in *Forbes*. 2017.

[16] Cooper, R.G. and E.J. Kleinschmidt, *New products: what separates winners from losers?* Journal of Product Innovation Management, 1987. **4**(3): p. 169–184.

[17] Van Westendorp, P.H. *NSS Price Sensitivity Meter (PSM): A new approach to study consumer perception of prices*. in *Proceedings of the 29th ESOMAR Congress*. 1976. Venice.

[18] Sadwick, R., *How To Price Your Product: A Guide To The Van Westendorp Pricing Model*, in *Forbes*. 2020.

[19] Sallis, J.E., et al., *Research Methods and Data Analysis for Business Decisions*, ed. Springer. 2021.

[20] Li, X., K.J. Li, and X. Wang, *Transparency of Behavior-Based Pricing*. Journal of Marketing Research, 2020. **57**(1): p. 78–99.

[21] Kübler, R., et al., *App popularity: Where in the world are consumers most sensitive to price and user ratings?* Journal of Marketing, 2018. **82**(5): p. 20–44.

[22] Khan, U. and R. Dhar, *Price-framing effects on the purchase of hedonic and utilitarian bundles*. Journal of Marketing Research, 2010. **47**(6): p. 1090–1099.

[23] Meyer, J., V. Shankar, and L.L. Berry, *Pricing hybrid bundles by understanding the drivers of willingness to pay*. Journal of the Academy of Marketing Science, 2018. **46**(3): p. 497–515.

https://doi.org/10.1515/9783110987102-013

[24] Derdenger, T. and V. Kumar, *The dynamic effects of bundling as a product strategy*. Marketing Science, 2013. **32**(6): p. 827–859.

[25] Yao, J. and H. Oppewal, *Unit pricing matters more when consumers are under time pressure*. European Journal of Marketing, 2016. **92**(1): p. 109–121.

[26] Gao, H., Y. Zhang, and V. Mittal, *How does local–global identity affect price sensitivity?* Journal of Marketing, 2017. **81**(3): p. 62–79.

[27] Hinterhuber, A., *Towards value-based pricing – An integrative framework for decision making*. Industrial Marketing Management, 2004. **33**(8): p. 765–778.

[28] Parguel, B., T. Delécolle, and P. Valette-Florence, *How price display influences consumer luxury perceptions*. Journal of Business Research, 2016. **69**(1): p. 341–348.

[29] Kapferer, J.-N. and G. Laurent, *Where do consumers think luxury begins? A study of perceived minimum price for 21 luxury goods in 7 countries*. Journal of Business Research, 2016. **69**(1): p. 332–340.

[30] Krämer, A., M. Jung, and T. Burgartz, *A small step from price competition to price war: understanding causes, effects and possible countermeasures*. International Business Research, 2016. **9**(3): p. 1–13.

[31] Rao, A.R., M.E. Bergen, and S. Davis, *How to fight a price war*. Harvard Business Review, 2000. **78**(2): p. 107–120.

[32] van Heerde, H.J., E. Gijsbrechts, and K. Pauwels, *Winners and losers in a major price war*. Journal of Marketing Research, 2008. **45**(5): p. 499–518.

[33] Kahneman, D., J.L. Knetsch, and R.H. Thaler, *Fairness and the assumptions of economics*. Journal of Business, 1986. **59**(4): p. 285–300.

[34] Xia, L., K.B. Monroe, and J.L. Cox, *The price is unfair! A conceptual framework of price fairness perceptions*. Journal of marketing, 2004. **68**(4): p. 1–15.

[35] Tarrahi, F., M. Eisend, and F. Dost, *A meta-analysis of price change fairness perceptions*. International Journal of Research in Marketing, 2016. **33**(1): p. 199–203.

[36] Guo, X. and B. Jiang, *Signaling through price and quality to consumers with fairness concerns*. Journal of Marketing Research, 2016. **53**(6): p. 988–1000.

[37] Lu, Z., et al., *The Price of Power: How Firm's Market Power Affects Perceived Fairness of Price Increases*. Journal of Retailing, 2019. **96**(1): p. 220–234.

[38] Shaddy, F. and L. Lee, *Price promotions cause impatience*. Journal of Marketing Research, 2020. **57**(1): p. 118–133.

[39] Guha, A., et al., *Reframing the discount as a comparison against the sale price: does it make the discount more attractive?* Journal of Marketing Research, 2018. **55**(3): p. 339–351.

[40] Alavi, S., et al., *The role of leadership in salespeople's price negotiation behavior*. Journal of the Academy of Marketing Science, 2018. **46**(4): p. 703–724.

[41] Keller, W.I., B. Deleersnyder, and K. Gedenk, *Price promotions and popular events*. Journal of Marketing, 2019. **83**(1): p. 73–88.

[42] Theotokis, A., K. Pramatari, and M. Tsiros, *Effects of Expiration Date-Based Pricing on Brand Image Perceptions*. Tsiros, Michael and Carrie Heilman (2005)," The Effect of Expiration Dates and Perceived Risks on Purchasing Behavior in Grocery Store Perishable Categories," Journal of Marketing, 2016. **69**(2): p. 114–129.

[43] Trump, R.K., *Harm in price promotions: when coupons elicit reactance*. Journal of Consumer Marketing, 2016. **33**(4): p. 302–310.

[44] Mamadehussene, S., *Price-matching guarantees as a direct signal of low prices*. Journal of Marketing Research, 2019. **56**(2): p. 245–258.

[45] Gordon-Hecker, T., et al., *Buy-one-get-one-free deals attract more attention than percentage deals*. Journal of Business Research, 2020. **111**: p. 128–134.

[46] Thaler, R., *Transaction Utility Theory*, in *NA – Advances in Consumer Research*, R.P. Bagozzi and A.M. Tybout, Editors. 1983, Association for Consumer Research: Ann Abor, MI. p. 229–232.

[47] Monroe, K.B. and A.Y. Lee, *Remembering versus knowing: Issues in buyers' processing of price information*. Journal of the Academy of Marketing Science, 1999. **27**(2): p. 207–225.

[48] Wieseke, J., A. Kolberg, and L.M. Schons, *Life could be so easy: the convenience effect of round price endings*. Journal of the Academy of Marketing Science, 2016. **44**(4): p. 474–494.

[49] Coulter, K.S., P. Choi, and K.B. Monroe, *Comma N'cents in pricing: The effects of auditory representation encoding on price magnitude perceptions*. Journal of Consumer Psychology, 2012. **22**(3): p. 395–407.

[50] Wadhwa, M. and K. Zhang, *This number just feels right: The impact of roundedness of price numbers on product evaluations*. Journal of Consumer Research, 2015. **41**(5): p. 1172–1185.

[51] Harms, C., et al., *Does it actually feel right? A replication attempt of the rounded price effect*. Royal Society open science, 2018. **5**(4): p. 1–13.

[52] Thomas, M., D.H. Simon, and V. Kadiyali, *The price precision effect: Evidence from laboratory and market data*. Marketing Science, 2010. **29**(1): p. 175–190.

[53] Janiszewski, C. and D. Uy, *Precision of the anchor influences the amount of adjustment*. Psychological Science, 2008. **19**(2): p. 121–127.

[54] Sokolova, T., S. Seenivasan, and M. Thomas, *The left-digit bias: when and why are consumers penny wise and pound foolish?* Journal of Marketing Research, 2020. **57**(4): p. 771–788.

[55] Barbera, M., et al., *Those prices are HOT! How temperature-related visual cues anchor expectations of price and value*. Journal of Retailing and Consumer Services, 2018. **44**(C): p. 178–181.

[56] Furnham, A. and H.C. Boo, *A literature review of the anchoring effect*. The journal of socio-economics, 2011. **40**(1): p. 35–42.

[57] Lin, C.-H. and J.-W. Wang, *Distortion of price discount perceptions through the left-digit effect*. Marketing Letters, 2017. **28**(1): p. 99–112.

[58] Puccinelli, N.M., et al., *Are men seduced by red? The effect of red versus black prices on price perceptions*. Journal of Retailing, 2013. **89**(2): p. 115–125.

[59] Karmarkar, U.R., B. Shiv, and B. Knutson, *Cost conscious? The neural and behavioral impact of price primacy on decision making*. Journal of Marketing Research, 2015. **52**(4): p. 467–481.

[60] Feng, S., et al., *Presenting comparative price promotions vertically or horizontally: Does it matter?* Journal of Business Research, 2017. **76**: p. 209–218.

[61] Tversky, A. and D. Kahneman, *Judgment under uncertainty: Heuristics and biases*. science, 1974. **185**(4157): p. 1124–1131.

[62] Yang, S.S., S.E. Kimes, and M.M. Sessarego, *Menu price presentation influences on consumer purchase behavior in restaurants*. International Journal of Hospitality Management, 2009. **28**(1): p. 157–160.

[63] Drèze, X. and J.C. Nunes, *Using combined-currency prices to lower consumers' perceived cost*. Journal of Marketing Research, 2004. **41**(1): p. 59–72.

[64] Mogilner, C. and J. Aaker, *"The time vs. money effect": Shifting product attitudes and decisions through personal connection*. Journal of Consumer Research, 2009. **36**(2): p. 277–291.

[65] Chandon, P. and N. Ordabayeva, *Supersize in one dimension, downsize in three dimensions: Effects of spatial dimensionality on size perceptions and preferences*. Journal of Marketing Research, 2009. **46**(6): p. 739–753.

[66] Brough, A.R. and A. Chernev, *When opposites detract: Categorical reasoning and subtractive valuations of product combinations*. Journal of Consumer Research, 2012. **39**(2): p. 399–414.

[67]   Kim, J., N. Novemsky, and R. Dhar, *Adding small differences can increase similarity and choice.* Psychological science, 2013. **24**(2): p. 225–229.

[68]   Prelec, D., G. Lowenstein, and O. Zellermeyer. *Closet Tightwads: Compulsive Reluctance to Spend and the Pain of Paying. Presented as part of a special session, Perceived Pain and Pleasure: Preferences for Experience-Structure and Characteristics.* in *NA – Advances in Consumer Research.* 1998. Provo, UT.

[69]   Gourville, J.T., *Pennies-a-day: The effect of temporal reframing on transaction evaluation.* Journal of Consumer Research, 1998. **24**(4): p. 395–408.

[70]   Abraham, A.T. and R.W. Hamilton, *When Does Partitioned Pricing Lead to More Favorable Consumer Preferences?: Meta-Analytic Evidence.* Journal of Marketing Research, 2018. **55**(5): p. 686–703.

[71]   Kahneman, D., J.L. Knetsch, and R.H. Thaler, *Experimental tests of the endowment effect and the Coase theorem.* Journal of political Economy, 1990. **98**(6): p. 1325–1348.

[72]   Mazumdar, T., S.P. Raj, and I. Sinha, *Reference price research: Review and propositions.* Journal of marketing, 2005. **69**(4): p. 84–102.

[73]   Soster, R.L., A.D. Gershoff, and W.O. Bearden, *The bottom dollar effect: the influence of spending to zero on pain of payment and satisfaction.* Journal of Consumer Research, 2014. **41**(3): p. 656–677.

[74]   Wathieu, L., A. Muthukrishnan, and B.J. Bronnenberg, *The asymmetric effect of discount retraction on subsequent choice.* Journal of Consumer Research, 2004. **31**(3): p. 652–657.

[75]   Tsiros, M. and D.M. Hardesty, *Ending a price promotion: retracting it in one step or phasing it out gradually.* Journal of Marketing, 2010. **74**(1): p. 49–64.

[76]   Dinerstein, M., et al., *Consumer price search and platform design in internet commerce.* American Economic Review, 2018. **108**(7): p. 1820–1859.

[77]   Acimovic, J., M. Lim, and H.-Y. Mak, *Beyond the speed-price tradeoff.* MIT Sloan Management Review, 2018. **59**(4): p. 13–15.

[78]   Kostyra, D.S., et al., *Decomposing the effects of online customer reviews on brand, price, and product attributes.* International Journal of Research in Marketing, 2016. **33**(1): p. 11–26.

[79]   Adaval, R. and K.B. Monroe, *Automatic construction and use of contextual information for product and price evaluations.* Journal of Consumer Research, 2002. **28**(4): p. 572–588.

[80]   Mehta, N., P. Detroja, and A. Agashe, *Amazon changes prices on its products about every 10 minutes – here's how and why they do it,* in *Business Insider.* 2018.

[81]   Dekimpe, M.G., *Retailing and retailing research in the age of big data analytics.* International Journal of Research in Marketing, 2020. **37**(1): p. 3–14.

[82]   NOU Norges offentlige utredninger, *Delingsøkonomien – muligheter og utfordringer.* 2017, Departementenes sikkerhets- og serviceorganisasjon. Informasjonsforvaltning.

[83]   Eckhardt, G.M., et al., *Marketing in the sharing economy.* Journal of Marketing, 2019. **83**(5): p. 5–27.

[84]   Haws, K.L., B. McFerran, and J.P. Redden, *The satiating effect of pricing: The influence of price on enjoyment over time.* Journal of Consumer Psychology, 2017. **27**(3): p. 341–346.

[85]   López-Fernández, A.M., *Price sensitivity versus ethical consumption: a study of millennial utilitarian consumer behavior.* Journal of Marketing Analytics, 2020. **8**(2): p. 57–68.

[86]   White, K., R. Habib, and D.J. Hardisty, *How to SHIFT consumer behaviors to be more sustainable: A literature review and guiding framework.* Journal of Marketing, 2019. **83**(3): p. 22–49.

About the Author

Professor Ragnhild Silkoset holds a doctoral degree in marketing strategy from BI Norwegian Business School in Oslo. She has written a well-received textbook on research methodology used by thousands of students. Her research focuses on pricing strategy, business-to-business marketing, market-oriented management, and marketing technology. Her research has been published in reputable international journals such as *Journal of Business Venturing*, *Business-to-Business Marketing*, *Journal of Business Ethics*, *International Journal of Bank Marketing*, *International Business Review*, and *European Journal of Marketing*, to mention just a few. She is a well-known expert in pricing in her home country and is frequently used as an expert witness in court, and as a pricing expert in national broadcast media. She is the founder and CEO of the consultancy company Pricing Decisions (see prisbeslutninger.no). She also holds an adjunct professor position at UiT The Arctic University of Norway, Tromsø.

https://doi.org/10.1515/9783110987102-014

List of Figures

https://doi.org/10.1515/9783110987102-015

List of Tables

https://doi.org/10.1515/9783110987102-016

Index

https://doi.org/10.1515/9783110987102-017

www.ingramcontent.com/pod-product-compliance
Lightning Source LLC
Chambersburg PA
CBHW061817210326
41599CB00034B/7030